DEEP LEARNING IN PRODUCTION

Sergios Karagiannakos

AI SUMMER

For online information and ordering of this and other AI Summer's books, please visit theaisummer.com.

Sergios Karagiannakos, AI Summer, sergios@theaisummer.com, Platanista 65, Sparta, Greece 23100

AI Summer, sergios@theaisummer.com, Platanista 65, Sparta, Greece 23100

ISBN: 978-618-00-3377-9

DEEP LEARNING IN
PRODUCTION

Table of Contents

Preface

Deep Learning in Production is a product of one year of effort. The pages and the code you will read, begun as articles on our blog AI Summer and they were later combined and organized into a single resource. Some were rewritten from scratch; some were modified to fit the book's structure and some they are entirely new.

The reason I decided to invest the time in writing this book is very simple. The practices and principles mentioned here is what I wish I knew when I started my journey on machine learning. Having an all-in guide that outlines every aspect of the deep learning pipeline would have accelerate my learning curve by a big margin. I do hope that it will do the same for you. Or at least, give you an overview of all the different components and steps, so you can have a holistic view of the field.

It accumulates the knowledge I have gained over the past years by working both as part of the machine learning infrastructure team at HubSpot, as a Data Scientist in a web agency, and as an independent contractor with various start-ups. Each project helped me learn something new and each team gave me a fresh and unique perspective on the field. This is what I hope to transmit to you.

The background and skills that you will acquire from this book will provide you better job opportunities, will differentiate you from other data scientists and machine learning researchers, and the most important thing: they will make you a better and more well-rounded engineer.

Thank you for choosing this book. I deeply appreciate it.

Sergios Karagiannakos

Acknowledgements

I am exceedingly grateful for everyone who helped and supported me in my journey to accumulate the knowledge that brought this book to you. That, of course, includes my family and friends.

Many special thanks I want to give to my co-student, lifelong friend and co-founder of AI Summer, Nikolas Adaloglou. The time that he spent in reviewing, rewriting and editing every single word of this book is truly invaluable. His excellent suggestions, unique perspective and tremendous patience make the book come alive. It wouldn't be possible without him.

I also want to express my gratitude to the amazing reviewers of this book, whose tips and suggestions were crucial. A huge shout out to Paris Koloveas, Michalis Goggolidis, Telemachos Chatzitheodorou and Konstantinos Poulinakis.

I couldn't forget, of course, all of AI Summer's readers who provide incredibly useful feedback on every article. Their persistence on constantly following our blog, reading our articles, and sharing our work is what motivates us to keep producing more content. Thank you.

Chapter 1

About this Book

In this chapter:

- What this book is about
- What do you need to know beforehand
- Who should read this book

1.1 Welcome to Deep Learning in Production

Hello. It's amazing to have you here. I'm super excited and you should be too. Deep Learning is one of the most transformative technologies of today. Deep neural networks are gradually changing many industries from healthcare and transportation to manufacturing and agriculture. However, the gap between creating a novel neural network architecture and using the model in an actual product is still quite large. The deployment of a machine learning model into production is where the fun begins. This is what this book is all about. **We will discuss the basic steps one should take to build, deploy, scale, and maintain deep learning models**.

1.2 Is this book for me?

Since you are here, I will probably say yes. But let's break it down. If you are interested in learning how to take a simple model and transform it into a real-world application, then the answer is absolutely yes.

Software engineers

If you come from a software engineering background and you are starting out with deep learning, you will learn how to apply the things you already know on AI projects.

Machine Learning researchers

If you don't have a programming background and you are a deep learning researcher or practitioner, you will familiarize yourself with the software development lifecycle. You will learn the basic principles of how to deploy and scale a machine learning application. In the end, you will be able to create an entirely new deep learning app from scratch and serve it to actual users.

Machine Learning engineers

If you are already a machine/deep learning engineer, you will solidify your understanding of the field, you will explore different practices and ideas, and you will familiarize yourself with software skills and technologies that you might have missed.

Data Scientists

If you are an experienced or aspiring Data Scientist, you will understand what it takes to productionize your models and to build customer-facing applications. You will comprehend the technical debt machine learning has, and you will gain a much broader image of the field.

1.3 What is the book's goal?

If I were to summarize the book into 4 sentences, I'd say that you will learn:

- how to structure and develop production-ready machine learning code
- how to optimize the model's performance and memory requirements
- how to make it available to the public by setting up a service on the cloud
- how to scale and maintain the service as the user base grows

1.4 Will this be difficult to learn?

To be honest with you, it won't be very easy. We cover some advanced concepts and technologies in this book, which might be hard to understand at first. We introduce a variety of frameworks and libraries that may have a steep learning curve. But don't be discouraged by that. As a machine learning engineer, no one expects you to be an expert on DevOps. However, having a basic understanding of all the systems and concepts, will get you a long way.

1.5 Why should you read this book?

The reason is very simple: because deep learning models are useless if they aren't applied in real-life applications. Don't get me wrong, research is awesome. No one enjoys creating a new fancy, state-of-the-art-model more than me. But the ultimate goal is usually to make the model visible to real users. And that's exactly what you'll learn here.

To clarify why Software Engineering is an undeniable significant part in deep learning, take for example Google Assistant. Behind Google Assistant is, without a doubt, an ingenious machine learning algorithm. But do you think that this amazing research alone is capable of answering the queries of millions of users at the same time? Absolutely not. There are dozens of software engineers behind the scenes, who maintain, optimize, and build the system. This is exactly what we are about to discover.

1.6 How to use this book?

This isn't going to be one of those high-level, abstract books that talk too much without practical value. Here we are going to dive deep into software, we will analyze details that may seem too low level, we will write a lot of code, and we will present the full deep learning development cycle from start to end.

Note, though, that all of the practices mentioned in this book are merely suggestions that come from my experience. Nothing will ever be declared as "the best way to do things".

There are many best practices that, in my opinion, will make your job much easier but that's up to each engineer to decide. After all, this is what makes our job so much fun. The ability to design and build things just the way we want.

Always remember that machine learning systems are not very mature yet, and new solutions and frameworks are created at a rapid pace.

1.7 How is the book structured?

Each chapter of the book will focus on a particular phase of the ML lifecycle.

We will:

1. Start from designing our end system.
2. Explore best practices on how to develop and structure deep learning code.
3. Dive more into the data pre-processing step.
4. Learn how to build optimized data pipelines.
5. Learn how to train models locally or in the cloud.
6. Build a first version of our deployable service.
7. Deploy it in a cloud instance.
8. Discover how to scale and maintain the system.
9. Close with existing end-to-end solutions and efforts to standardize the entire lifecycle.

It's going to be a long but amazing journey.

1.8 Do I need to know anything else before I get started?

Needless to say, that in order to follow along, you will need to have a solid background on programming and/or machine learning.

We will use Tensorflow 2.0 in order to showcase the different techniques and ideas. So, a good understanding of Tensorflow would be ideal. However, all the principles apply to other frameworks such as Pytorch, MXNet and CNTK.

Besides Tensorflow, here is a list of other frameworks and tools that will use throughout the book: Flask, uWSGI, Nginx, Docker, Kubernetes, Google Cloud. As you have probably guessed, this book is quite opinionated in terms of libraries. You can find links with the documentation of all mentioned libraries in the Appendix.

But make no mistake, the choice of the particular tools is only to showcase the concepts. In your own projects, you are of course free to use whatever you like. Along the process, I will also give you some extra tips to better utilize the tools, increase your productivity and enhance your workflow.

Without further ado, let's get started.

Chapter 2

Designing a Machine Learning System

In this chapter:

- How to design a deep learning application
- What questions do you need to answer
- What are the different phases of machine learning development

The most important step in any software project is the design phase. Gathering requirements, understanding the business domain, and designing a viable and scalable solution. Machine learning systems are no different. However, one might argue that they are more complicated than normal software because of the many moving parts: data, models and code are always changing during the system's lifecycle.

2.1 Machine learning: phase zero

Before writing a single line of code, it is vital to develop a full solution in paper. That's what I like to call phase zero. During phase zero, the first priority is to gather requirements. Here are some questions we need to answer:

- What problem do we want to solve using Machine Learning?
- Is Machine Learning the best approach?

- What domain knowledge is necessary to proceed?
- How will we acquire data for the model?
- How will we pre-process the data and on what scale?
- How many people do we need?
- Do we have a timeline for the project?
- Where will the model be trained?
- How will the model be deployed?
- How will we be able to scale it as the user base grows?
- How will we maintain it?
- Is it an offline or online system?
- How will we test the system?
- Can we reproduce the results?
- Can we repeat the lifecycle from scratch if needed?
- How can we evaluate the success of our system?

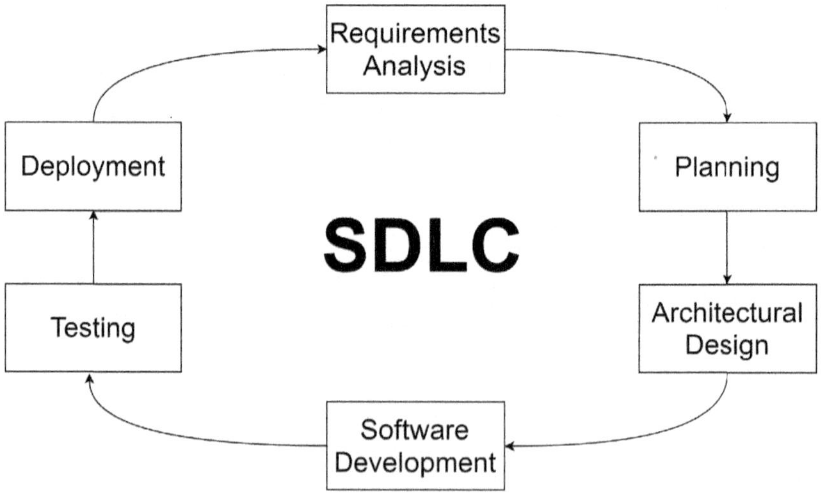

Figure 2.1: Software Development lifecycle

And many more. All the answers need to be as accurate as possible but always with the ability to be altered during the process. In other words, an ML system should follow the Software Development Life Cycle (SDLC) as it has been established over the years.

Assuming that we gathered the requirements and we fully understood the problem, let's now look closer at the software aspect of an ML system lifecycle. Typically, we can split an ML system into 3 parts: Data, Model and DevOps.

2.2 Data engineering

Data is arguably the most fundamental piece of an ML workflow. Data engineering refers to the process of gathering data, exploring them, and transforming them before they are fed into the model.

A common approach looks something like this:

1. **Data sources identification**: First, we need to find out where we will get our data from, and how we can query from those sources.
2. **Data aggregation**: This involves accumulating data from many sources and building a single source, whether this is a data lake, a data warehouse, a simple database, a cloud bucket or a single csv file.
3. **Data augmentation**: Due to lack of enough data or to improve the model's accuracy, we often extend the dataset by generating new datapoints.
4. **Data exploration**: Here we gather statistics of our data, detect outliers/anomalies, uncover insights and identify patterns.
5. **Data labelling**: Models that require some sort of supervised training also require labels in our data.
6. **Data validation**: Validation usually happens with the help of a pre-generated schema, which can help us clean the data.
7. **Data transformation**: Before we feed the data into a model, we need to preprocess and transform them into the desired format.
8. **Data ingestion**: Finally. the data should be injected into the model either for training or inference.

Data engineering comes with a lot of challenges that mostly concern the scale of the data. Especially in deep learning where we have huge amounts of data, we need to make sure that these steps can be performed seamlessly. This typically involves solutions such as distributed databases, distributed data loading, parallel processing, etc. Luckily, data engineering has been a well-studied field and there are many powerful architectures out there that tackle these issues.

2.3 Model engineering

Model engineering on the other hand is a much newer field with not many standard solutions yet. But we're slowly getting there. The machine learning model's lifecycle starts from R&D and finishes with the model deployment:

1. **Prototyping**: A data scientist will experiment with different types of models, will figure out the math, and build the first prototype. This usually happens in a notebook or in a local IDE.

2. **Training**: Models need to be trained on a dataset either locally or in the cloud. Hardware accelerators like GPUs and TPUs have their own special place in this step.

3. **Evaluation**: Evaluating the model's performance comes after training. Here we ensure that it indeed addresses the business problem.

4. **Benchmarking**: Setting a baseline model that will be used to compare future iterations with.

5. **Tuning**: Hypepamater tuning and tweaks in the architecture sometimes occur after evaluation.

6. **Integration**: Checking that the model is actually servable from the infrastructure to make sure that no bad models will be pushed.

7. **Versioning**: A simple form of version control can also be in place to enable deployment rollbacks and performance comparisons with future models.

8. **Packaging**: Before deployment, we usually serialize the model into a compact and lightweight format.

The above workflow might vary depending the application. For example, offline learning differs significantly from online learning where the model is retrained frequently. Batch predictions are sometimes supported as well. That's why there is no golden workflow for every system. It is up to the engineers to find the one that suits their needs to the maximum.

2.4 DevOps engineering

Deployment is the stage which most ML engineers and data scientists are less familiar with. Like every software project, a machine learning application must be highly scalable, reliable, and always available. DevOps has made huge achievements over the last few years. However, in ML, things aren't that clear yet. The DevOps pipeline in terms of machine learning usually looks like the following:

1. **Model pushing**: This is where the trained model is being pushed into production, whether this is an edge device, a web service, or a decentralized application.
2. **Monitoring**: The model should always be monitored in terms of accuracy and speed. The same is true for the serving infrastructure in terms of reliability and availability. This typically is accomplished by rich visualizations, a logging system, and alerts for unexpected incidents.
3. **Scaling**: As the user base grows, scaling the app and ensuring that everything works as expected is vital.

2.5 Putting it all together

Taking all that into consideration is by no means an easy task. The truth is that machine learning systems (or deep learning for that matter) are inherently complex and require careful examination of all the subcomponents, before the development phase. The even trickier part is that this is not an one-time effort. Most of the pipeline's components will be executed over and over in an iterative form. Why? Because data are changing. The model's accuracy is falling. The infrastructure does not scale well. That's why design is so important. In my experience, the lack of careful design is the most prominent reason why ML projects fail.

By the way, MLOps is a relatively new term that describes the effort to build an end-to-end system that takes care of all the aforementioned steps of the pipeline. But more on that in the final chapter. Until then, we need to dive into each individual component, and see below the surface in order to understand how to build and deploy deep learning systems.

2.6 Tackling a real-life problem

For a better comprehension of the principles and ideas, we will deal with a real-life problem throughout the book. We will take a simple Tensorflow model, and we will build upon this in order to construct a deployable and scalable application. So, the entire book will be an effort to productionize this standard ML code into a fully-fledged application. On each chapter, we will gradually enhance our code and experiment with different libraries and concepts. Keep in mind that you don't have to use everything in your project. Here, we will just showcase the different libraries to help you make better decisions when you design your own ML app. Having said that, let's explore our real-life scenario.

We assume that we are right after the experimentation phase of ML, and we have already developed a model. As a basis, we will use a U-Net that performs semantic segmentation. **Our end goal is to build a web application. The user/client will be able to send a request with an image over the web and we will return the segmentation mask of the image**.

For those who are not very familiar with UNets and image segmentation , let's clarify a few things.

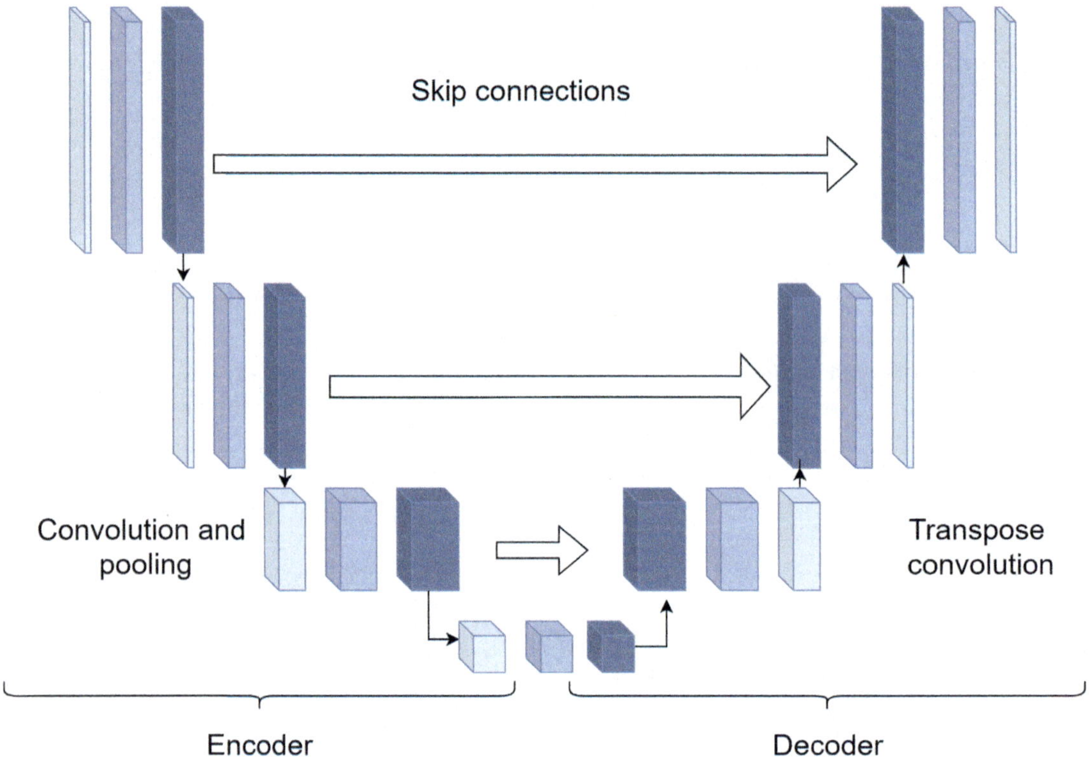

Figure 2.2: A UNet model

Semantic segmentation is the task of assigning a label to every pixel of an image based on its context. This is super useful because it enables computers to understand what they see. I'm confident you can think of many applications that this would be helpful. Some of them include autonomous cars, robotics and medical imaging.

A well-known model that is used in image segmentation, are UNets. UNets are symmetric convolutional neural networks that consist of an encoder and a decoder. The main architectural design of a UNet is that every layer of the encoder connects with a layer of the decoder via skip connections. Often, for every encoder layer we have another decoder layer. The encoder layer halves the spatial dimensions of an image and double its channels, while the decoder is operating in the opposite manner. The result is to have a U-shaped network, hence their name.

You can find our starting code below:

```
import tensorflow as tf
from tensorflow_examples.models.pix2pix import pix2pix

base_model = tf.keras.applications.MobileNetV2(
    input_shape=[128, 128, 3], include_top=False
    )

# Use the activations of these layers
layer_names = [
    'block_1_expand_relu',    # 64x64
    'block_3_expand_relu',    # 32x32
    'block_6_expand_relu',    # 16x16
    'block_13_expand_relu',   # 8x8
    'block_16_project',       # 4x4
]
layers = [base_model.get_layer(name).output for name in layer_names]

# Create the feature extraction model
down_stack = tf.keras.Model(inputs=base_model.input, outputs=layers)
down_stack.trainable = False
up_stack = [
    pix2pix.upsample(512, 3),  # 4x4 -> 8x8
    pix2pix.upsample(256, 3),  # 8x8 -> 16x16
    pix2pix.upsample(128, 3),  # 16x16 -> 32x32
    pix2pix.upsample(64, 3),   # 32x32 -> 64x64
]

def unet_model(output_channels):
  inputs = tf.keras.layers.Input(shape=[128, 128, 3])
  x = inputs

  # Downsampling through the model
  skips = down_stack(x)
  x = skips[-1]
  skips = reversed(skips[:-1])

  # Upsampling and establishing the skip connections
  for up, skip in zip(up_stack, skips):
    x = up(x)
```

```
        concat = tf.keras.layers.Concatenate()

        x = concat([x, skip])

    # This is the last layer of the model
    last = tf.keras.layers.Conv2DTranspose(
        output_channels, 3, strides=2,
        padding='same')  #64x64 -> 128x128
    x = last(x)

    return tf.keras.Model(inputs=inputs, outputs=x)
```

Let's analyse it a bit. As you can see, our model is a modified UNet model. A pretrained `MobileNetV2` is used as the encoder and a `Pix2pix` model as the decoder. The encoder downsamples the input images and it will not be trained during the training process. The decoder, on the other hand, is a stack of upsampling layers with skip connections. The final layer is a `Conv2DTranspose` module that will convert the output of the decoder to the size of the input.

I won't go into more details about the model because it's not the subject of the book. However, feel free to spend some time here to fully understand every code line if you like. Our goal is to use the code as a basis as we move along. Now that we have the first iteration of our model, it's time to proceed with the remaining software lifecycle.

Note that you can find the entire code mentioned in this book under the `The-AI-Summer/Deep-Learning-In-Production` Github repository. The code is split by chapter so as to be easier to follow along.

Chapter 3

Setting up a Deep Learning Workstation

In this chapter:

- What to do before starting the development of a deep learning project
- What tools and libraries you can use
- How to set up your workstation

The first step before building a deep learning application is to properly set up our development workstation. In this chapter, we will discuss some basic requirements for our personal computer's hardware and software in order to be able to follow along throughout this book. We will also explore popular tools and libraries, used by many machine learning engineers around the world, to improve productivity. Note that all these are only suggestions and that each developer is able to choose their own preferred software and hardware.

The reasons I included this section are a) to give you an idea of how most software engineers work, b) to present some best practices that are proven to improve collaboration and productivity and c) to make sure that each one of you will be able to replicate and run our application in your own laptop with no additional problems.

3.1 Laptop setup

"Laptop" is used here as a generic term that represents the personal computing system. Each engineer has their own preference. Some prefer to work on an 11-inch laptop, some on a custom-build PC, and some on a very powerful high-end workstation. The following software and hardware suggestions are valid regardless of your choice.

3.1.1 Laptop requirements

It is usually recommended to have a powerful PC with a strong GPU in order to be able to train machine learning models, but this is not necessarily true as we will see down the road. Deep learning training can also be executed in a remote environment utilizing the cloud. But having a good GPU, a decent CPU and enough memory will certainly save you some bucks. And it is definitely not essential to buy a $5,000 laptop just for your deep learning needs.

Most of the times, an NVIDIA GPU with 4GB VRAM, an 8-core CPU and a 16 GB system memory will be sufficient enough (at least at the time of writing this book). If I had to choose to upgrade one of those, I would probably go with a higher-end GPU.

3.1.2 Operating system

In terms of what operating system to choose, I will dare to say that Ubuntu, macOS, and Windows will serve you well in most of cases. Keep in mind that with the latter one, you may need to spend more time setting things up and it may cause some small inconveniences in particular cases. But it is definitely possible to do everything on a Windows machine. My personal choice to develop the code for this book, train the model and deploy the web application, was Ubuntu 20.04.01 LTS (Focal Fossa).

Tip: If you are on a Windows 10 machine, WSL (Windows Subsystem for Linux) is something you should be aware of, as it brings a complete Linux terminal interface inside Windows. It may come with some caveats and limitations, but you will be capable of installing and executing most of the things in this book.

3.2 Frameworks and libraries

Here we'll discover a complete list of all the frameworks and libraries we will use in this book in order to have a clear idea of what is coming, and to give you the time to install and configure some or all of them. The list extends from deep learning-specific open-source libraries to DevOps frameworks:

- **Python**: Python is the go-to language for machine learning nowadays and it has a rather complete ecosystem of related libraries (the code presented in this book is in Python 3.7).

- **Tensorflow**: Tensorflow is the most popular end-to-end framework for building and deploying deep learning architectures. It is maintained by Google and it was released in 2015. Note that we use Tensorflow 2.0, which also includes Keras as part of the basic library.

- **Numpy**: Numpy is a Python library for performing operations between large, multidimensional arrays. It supports sophisticated mathematical functions and a wide set of linear algebra operations.

- **Flask**: Flask is a micro web framework written in Python for building web applications.

- **uWSGI**: uWSGI is a web server framework to run Python web applications.

- **Nginx**: Nginx is a high-performant HTTP server and reverse proxy.

- **Docker**: Docker is a set of Platform-as-a-Service (PaaS) products to deliver software in packages called containers.

- **Kubernetes**: Kubernetes is a container-orchestration system for automating computer application deployment, scaling, and management.

- **Google Cloud**: Google Cloud platform is a suite of cloud computing services that run and are maintained on Google's infrastructure.

If you own an Nvidia GPU, you might also need to install CUDA. CUDA is a parallel programming framework that allows developers to program on GPUs. More specifically, you will need to install the Nvidia GPU drivers, the CUDA toolkit as well as cuDNN in order to be able to train your Tensorflow models in a graphics processing unit. Don't forget that you have to install a Tensorflow version with GPU support. The official docs do a great job in explaining the process, so I trust that you won't encounter many problems.

3.3 Development tools

In this section, I will suggest some development tools I use daily, which I think will make your programming life a lot easier, and will help you write code faster and more efficiently. Note that they are merely suggestions and you shouldn't feel obligated by any means to follow along. Since there are tens of alternatives, feel free to use whatever tools and libraries you're more comfortable with.

3.3.1 Terminal

I highly recommend installing `zsh` instead of `bash`. The default Linux shell is bash and of course you will be totally fine with it. MacOS, though, has already chose `zsh` as the default shell. `zsh` is an extension that comes with some cool features such as line completion, spelling correction, command history.

Note that instead of using `homebrew` as you would do on a mac, you can use `apt-get` to download it, which is the standard packaging system in most Linux distributions. You can also take advantage of its amazing plugins such as `zsh-syntax-highlighting` and `zsh-autosuggestions`. Zsh will definitely come in handy when you want to switch Python virtual environments or when you're working with git and different branches. In the Figure 3.1, you can see how I set up my terminal (which is pretty minimal).

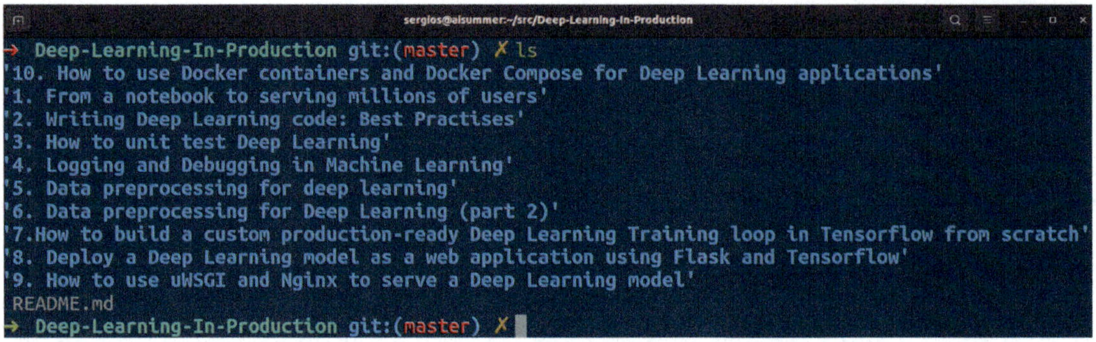

Figure 3.1: Example of a Linux terminal

After setting up the terminal, it's time to download some basic software. Git is the first one in our list.

3.3.2 Version control

Git is an open-source version control system and is essential if you work with other developers on the same codebase. It lets you track who changed what, revert the code to a previous state, and allow multiple people to change the same file. Git is used by the majority of developers nowadays and is probably the single most important tool in the list.

You can install and configure git using the following commands:

```
$ sudo apt-get install git

#configure git account
```

```
$ git config --global user.name "AI Summer"
$ git config --global user.email "sergios@theaisummer.com"
```

You can also use GitHub to save your code and collaborate with other engineers. GitHub is a great tool to review code, track what you need to do, and make sure that you won't lose your code no matter what. To be able to use it, you will need to set up a ssh key so you can commit and push code from the terminal. Personally, I use both git and GitHub pretty much in all my projects (even if I'm the only developer).

```
#to create the key
$ ssh-keygen -t rsa -C your_name@github.com

#to copy to your keyboard
$ cat  ~/.ssh/id_rsa.pub
```

Then go to your GitHub account in the browser -> Account settings -> ssh keys and add the ssh key you just copied.

Finally, run the below command to make sure everything went well.

```
$ ssh -T git@github.com
```

I also recommend GitHub Desktop to interact with GitHub using a GUI and not the command line, as it can sometimes be quite tedious.

Tip: GitHub Desktop doesn't have a Linux version, but there is an awesome open-source repo `shiftkey/desktop` that works perfectly fine and it's what I personally use.

3.4 Python package and environment management

In order to isolate our deep learning environment from the rest of our system and to be able to test different library releases, virtual environments are the solution. **Virtual environments let us isolate the python installation with all the libraries that will be needed for a project**. That way we can have, for example, both Python 2.7 and 3.6 on the same machine. A good rule of thumb is to have a separate environment per project.

One of the most popular Python distributions out there is Anaconda. It is widely used by many data scientists and machine learning engineers, as it **comes prebaked with a number of popular ML libraries and tools. Moreover, it natively supports virtual environments**. It also comes with a package manager (called `conda`) and a GUI as a way to manipulate libraries from there instead of the command line. You can install the `miniconda` version, which includes only the necessary stuff, as you may don't want your laptop to be cluttered with unnecessary libraries. However, the full version is perfectly fine as well.

```
# download miniconda
$ wget https://repo.anaconda.com/miniconda/Miniconda2-latest
-Linux-x86_64.sh

# install
$ ./sh Miniconda2-latest-Linux-x86_64.sh
```

At this point, we would normally create a `conda` environment and install some basic Python libraries, but we won't. This is because in the next step, PyCharm will create one for us automatically.

3.4.1 IDE / code editor

This is where many developers can become very opinionated on which IDE/editor is the best. In my experience, it doesn't really matter which one to use as long as it can increase your productivity and help you write and debug code faster. You can choose between Visual Studio Code, Atom, Emacs, Vim, PyCharm and more. In my case, PyCharm seems more natural as it provides some out of the box functionalities, such as integration with `git` and `conda`, unit testing, plugins, and bash support.

Tip: When you create a project, PyCharm will ask you to select your Python interpreter. In this step, you can choose to create a new `conda` environment and the IDE will find your `conda` installation and create one for you without doing anything else. It will also **automatically activate it every time you are starting the integrated terminal**.

I am going to use Python 3.7.7 so if you want to follow along, it would be better if we have the same version (any 3.7.x should work).

Once you create your project and create your conda environment, you will probably want to install some Python libraries. There are two ways to do that:

1. Open the terminal and run `conda install library` inside your environment.
2. Go to File → Settings→ Project → Project Interpreter and install from here using PyCharm.

Another cool feature of PyCharm is that it contains an integrated version control functionality (VCS). It will detect your git configuration in your project (if exists) and it will give you the ability to commit, pull, push and even open a PR (pull

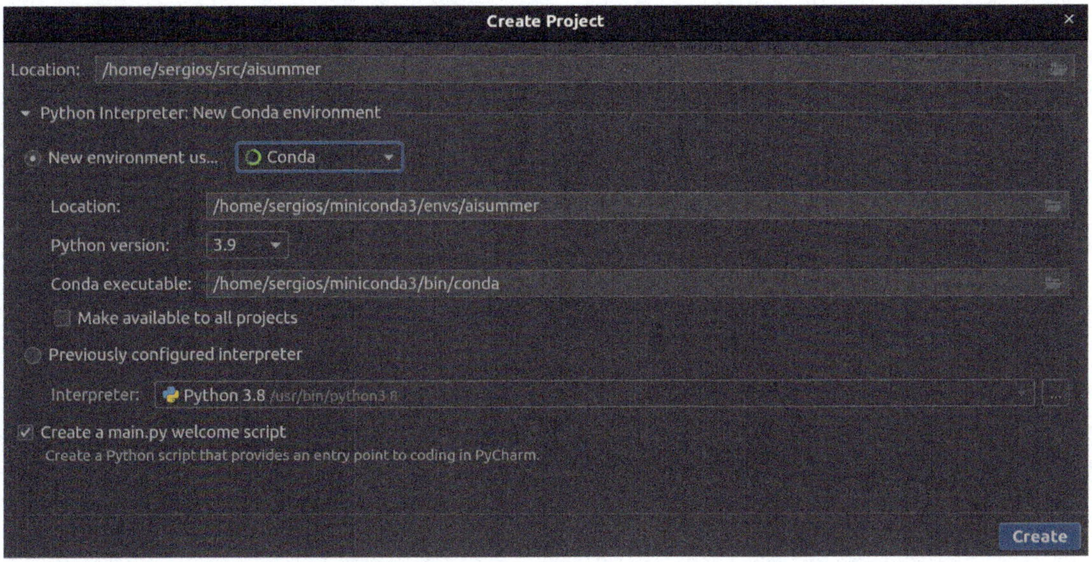

Figure 3.2: Project creation on Pycharm

request) from the VCS menu tab (in case you don't want to use either the terminal or GitHub Desktop).

3.4.2 Other tools

Other tools which you might want to use, especially if you are part of a team are:

- **Slack** is a very good tool to communicate with your team. And it comes with a plethora of integrations such as GitHub and Google Calendar.
- **Zenhub** is a project management tool, specifically designed for GitHub. Since it's not free, a very good alternative is the built-in project functionality inside GitHub.
- **Zoom** for video calls and meetings.
- **Lucidchart** is a platform that allows users to collaborate on drawing, revising and sharing charts and diagrams (very useful for software system designs).

Now we are all set. Our laptop is rock solid, our environment is (almost) ready for deep learning development, and our tools are installed and properly configured.

My favourite time is here: Time to write some code!

Chapter 4

Writing and Structuring Deep Learning Code

In this chapter:

- What are some best practices when writing deep learning code
- How to unit test your code
- How to debug your code

This chapter is all about the development of a production-ready deep learning project. We will start off by examining deep learning coding examples from a software engineering perspective. Afterwards, we will discuss best practices that you can follow when writing code, as well as the tools to include in your arsenal to incorporate these practices.

4.1 Best practices

When referring to best practices, we usually talk about a set of "rules" one should follow. The word "rules" is in quotation marks because these aren't exactly rules. They are well-established guidelines and workflows that many teams have successfully used before and they all indirectly agree that it's the best way of doing things. However, notice that some of these practices come from my own experience and might not resonate with you. In that case, feel free to disregard them.

4.1.1 Project structure

One very important aspect when writing code is how we structure our project. A good structure should obey the "**Separation of concerns**" principle in terms that **each functionality should be a distinct component**. In this way, it can be easily modified and extended without breaking other parts of the code. Moreover, it can be reused in many places without the need to write duplicate code.

Tip: Writing the same code once is perfect, twice is kind of fine but thrice it's not. DRY (Don't Repeat Yourself) is a commonly used acronym that developers use to indicate that a piece of code or a specific functionality is not duplicated. (e.g. we should DRY this function)

The way I like to organize most of my deep learning projects is something like that:

```
$ tree -L 1
.
|------configs
|------dataloader
|------evaluation
|------executor
|------model
|------notebooks
|------ops
|------utils
```

And that, of course, is my personal preference. Feel free to play around with this until you find what suits you best.

Python modules and packages

Notice that in the project structure that I presented, each folder is a separate module that can be imported into other modules just by writing `import module`. Here, we should make a quick distinction between what python calls **module** and what **package**.

A module is simply a `.py` file containing Python code. A package, however, is like a directory that holds sub-packages and modules. In order for a package to be importable, it should contain an `__init__.py` file (even if it's empty). That is not the case for modules. In our case, each folder is a package and it contains an `__init__.py` file.

In our example, we have 8 different packages:

1. **configs**: In this module, we define everything that can be configurable and can be changed in the future. Good examples are training hyperparameters, folder paths, metrics, flags, etc.

2. **dataloader** is quite self-explanatory. All the data loading and data pre-processing classes and functions live here.

3. **evaluation** is a collection of code files that aims to evaluate the performance and accuracy of our model.

4. **executor**: in this folder, we usually have all the functions and scripts that train the model or use it for prediction in different environments. And by different environments, I mean executors for CPU-only systems, executors for GPUs, executors for distributed systems. This package is our connection with the outer world and it's what our `main.py` will use.

5. **model** contains the actual deep learning code (we are talking about Tensorflow, Pytorch, etc).

6. **notebooks** include all our Jupyter/Colab notebooks in one place that we built in the experimentation phase of the machine learning lifecycle.

7. **ops**: This one is not always needed, as it includes operations not related with machine learning such as algebraic transformations, image manipulation techniques or maybe graph operations.

8. **utils**: Utility functions that are used in more than one place. In essence, everything that doesn't belong in the pre-described categories comes here.

4.1.2 Object-oriented programming

Now that we have our project well-structured, we can begin to discover how our code should look like on a lower level.

The answer to that question is **classes** and everything that comes with this. Admittedly, **Object-Oriented Programming (OOP)** might not be the first thing that comes to mind when writing Python code (it definitely is when coding in Java or C#), but you will be surprised by how easy it is to develop software when thinking in objects.

Tip: A good way to code your way is to try and write Python the same way you would write Java.

Yes, I know that's not your usual advice, but you'll understand what I mean in time. If we reprogram the UNet model, presented in Chapter 2.6, in an object-oriented way, the result would be something like this:

```python
class UNet():

    def __init__(self, config):
        self.base_model = tf.keras.applications.MobileNetV2(
           input_shape = self.config.model.input, include_top=False
        )
        self.batch_size = self.config.train.batch_size
        . . .

    def load_data(self):
        """Loads and Preprocess data """
        self.dataset, self.info =
            DataLoader().load_data(self.config.data)
        self._preprocess_data()

    def _preprocess_data(self):
        . . .

    def _set_training_parameters(self):
        . . .

    def _normalize(self, input_image, input_mask):
       . . .

    def _load_image_train(self, datapoint):
       . . .

    def _load_image_test(self, datapoint):
        . . .

    def build(self):
        """ Builds the Keras model based """
        layer_names = [
            'block_1_expand_relu',   # 64x64
            'block_3_expand_relu',   # 32x32
            'block_6_expand_relu',   # 16x16
            'block_13_expand_relu',   # 8x8
            'block_16_project',   # 4x4
        ]
        layers =
```

```
            [self.base_model.get_layer(name).output for name
            in layer_names]

        . . .

        self.model = tf.keras.Model(inputs=inputs, outputs=x)

    def train(self):
        . . .

    def evaluate(self):
        . . .
```

If you compare the new code with the original one, you will start to understand what these practices accomplish.

Basically, you can see that **the model is a class, each separate functionality is encapsulated within a method, and all the common variables are declared as instance variables.**

As you can easily realize, it becomes much easier to alter the training functionality of our model, to change the layers or to flip the default of a boolean variable. On the other hand, writing spaghetti code (which is a programming slang for chaotic code) is something that should be avoided. Because it is much more difficult to find the responsibility of each function, or if a change affects other parts of the code, or how to debug the software.

As a result, we get free **maintainability, extensibility, and simplicity**.

Abstraction and Inheritance

However, using classes and objects give us a lot more than that. Abstraction and inheritance are two of the most important topics in OOP.

By using **abstraction** we can declare the desired functionalities without dealing with how they are going to be implemented. To this end, we can first think about the logic behind our code and then dive into programming every single part of it. The same pattern can easily be adopted in deep learning code. To better understand what I'm saying, have a look at the code below:

```
class BaseModel(ABC):
    """Abstract Model class that is inherited to all models"""
    def __init__(self, cfg):
        self.config = Config.from_json(cfg)
```

```python
    @abstractmethod
    def load_data(self):
        pass

    @abstractmethod
    def build(self):
        pass

    @abstractmethod
    def train(self):
        pass

    @abstractmethod
    def evaluate(self):
        pass
```

One can easily observe that the **functions have no body**. They are just a declaration. In the same logic, you can think of every functionality you are going to need, declare it as an abstract method or class, and you are done. It's like having a contract of what the code should look like. That way you can decide first on the high-level implementation and then tackle each part in detail.

Consequently, that contract can now be used by other classes that will "extend" our abstract class. This is called **inheritance** . The base class will be inherited in the "child" class and it will immediately define its structure. So, the new class is obligated to have all the abstract functions as well. Of course, it can also have many other functions, not declared in the abstract class.

Look below how we pass the `BaseModel` class as an argument in the `UNet`. That's all we need. Also in our case, we need to call the `__init__` function of the parent class, which we accomplish with the `super()`. `super` is a special Python function that calls the constructor (the function that initializes the object aka the `__init__`) of the parent class. The rest of the code is normal deep learning code.

The main way to have abstraction in Python is by using the ABC library.

```python
class UNet(BaseModel):
    """Unet Model class. Contains functionality for building,
    training and evaluating the model"""


    def __init__(self, config):
```

```
        super().__init__(config)
        self.base_model = tf.keras.applications.MobileNetV2(
            input_shape=self.config.model.input, include_top=False
        )

       . . .

    def load_data(self):
        self.dataset, self.info =
            DataLoader().load_data(self.config.data )
        self._preprocess_data()

        . . .

    def build(self):

        . . .

        self.model = tf.keras.Model(inputs=inputs, outputs=x)

    def train(self):
        self.model.compile(
            optimizer = self.config.train.optimizer.type
            loss = tf.keras.losses.SparseCategoricalCrossentropy(
                from_logits = True
            ),
            metrics = self.config.train.metrics
        )

        model_history = self.model.fit(
            self.train_dataset,
            epochs = self.epoches,
            steps_per_epoch = self.steps_per_epoch,
            validation_steps = self.validation_steps,
            validation_data=self.test_dataset
        )

        return model_history.history['loss'],model_history
            .history['val_loss']

    def evaluate(self):
```

```python
        predictions = []
        for image, mask in self.dataset.take(1):
            predictions.append(self.model.predict(image))

        return predictions
```

Moreover, you can imagine that the base class can be inherited by many children (that's called **polymorphism**). That way we can have many models with the same base model as a parent but with different logic. In another practical aspect, if a new developer joins our team, he can easily find out what his code should look like just by inheriting our abstract class.

Static and class methods

Static and class methods are two interesting patterns that can simplify and make our code less error-prone. In OOP, we have the class and the instances. **The class is like the blueprint for creating objects. Instances are the actual objects that have the class as type.**

Class methods take as arguments the actual class and they are usually used as constructors for creating new instances of the class. You will understand what this means in the next paragraphs where we present some coding examples.

Static methods are methods that refer only to the class, not its instances, and they will not modify the class state. Static methods are mostly used for utility functions that aren't going to change.

Definition: The class state of an object is the values of all its variables.

Let's see how they can be applied in our code:

The below code snippet constructs a config from a json file. The **classmethod** `from_json` returns an actual instance of the `Config` class created from a json file by calling `Config.from_json(json_file)`. In other words, it is a constructor of our class. By doing this, we can have multiple constructors for the same class (we might for example want to create a config using a yaml file).

```python
class Config:
    """
      Config class which contains data, train and model
      hyperparameters
    """

    def __init__(self, data, train, model):
```

```python
        self.data = data
        self.train = train
        self.model = model

    @classmethod
    def from_json(cls, cfg):
        """Creates config from json"""
        params = json.loads(
            json.dumps(cfg), object_hook=HelperObject
        )
        return cls(params.data, params.train, params.model)
```

Static methods, on the other hand, are methods that are called on the actual object and not an instance of it. A perfect example is the `DataLoader` class, where we load the data from an external URL. Is there a reason to have a new `DataLoader` instance? Not really, because everything is stable in this functionality and nothing will ever change. When states are changing, it is better to class instances and instance methods.

```python
class DataLoader:
    """Data Loader class. Loads the data as a tfds dataset"""

    @staticmethod
    def load_data(data_config):
        """Loads dataset from path"""
        return tfds.load(
            data_config.path, with_info=data_config.load_with_info
        )
```

4.1.3 Configuration

Configuration files (commonly known as config files) are files used to configure the parameters and initial settings for computer programs. They differ in syntax and format but most of them are very readable and easily modifiable.

It is generally recommended to have all settings in a single place so they can be changed seamlessly. As an example, take a look on the config file below:

```python
CFG = {
    "data": {
        "path": "oxford_iiit_pet:3.*.*",
        "image_size": 128,
```

```
        "load_with_info": True
    },
    "train": {
        "batch_size": 64,
        "buffer_size": 1000,
        "epoches": 20,
        "val_subsplits": 5,
        "optimizer": {
            "type": "adam"
        },
        "metrics": ["accuracy"]
    },
    "model": {
        "input": [128, 128, 3],
        "up_stack": {
            "layer_1": 512,
            "layer_2": 256,
            "layer_3": 128,
            "layer_4": 64,
            "kernels": 3
        },
        "output": 3
    }
}
```

Whenever we want to change the batch size of our data, the optimization algorithm or the number of nodes in a layer, we can immediately come here.

4.1.4 Type checking

Another cool and useful feature, borrowed again from Java, is type checking. Type checking is the process of verifying and enforcing the constraints of types. And by types we mean whether a variable is a string, an integer or an object. To be more precise, in Python we have **type hints**. Python doesn't support type checking, because it is a dynamically typed language. But we will see how to get around that. Type checking is essential because it can acknowledge bugs and errors very early and can help us write better code overall.

It is very common when coding in Python to have moments where you wonder if a particular variable is a string or an integer. And you find yourself tracking it throughout the code trying to figure out what type it is. And that's much trickier to do when that code is implemented with Tensorflow or Pytorch.

A very simple way to do type checking can be seen below:

```
def ai_summer_func(x:int) -> int:
    return x+5
```

As you can see, we declare that both x and the function's return value should be of type integer.

Note that this will not throw an error on an exception. It is just a suggestion. IDEs like PyCharm (or Python linters) will automatically discover them and show a warning. That way we can easily detect bugs and fix them as we are building our code.

If we want to catch these kinds of errors, we can use a static type checker like `Pytype`. After installing it and including our type hints in our code, we can run something like below and it will show us all the type errors in our code. `Pytype` is used in many Tensorflow official codebases and it's a Google library. An example can be illustrated below:

```
$ pytype main.py

File "/home/aisummer/PycharmProjects/Deep-Learning-Production-Course
/main.py", line 19, in <module>: Function ai_summer_func was called
with the wrong arguments [wrong-arg-types]
  Expected: (x: int)
  Actually passed: (x: str)
```

One important thing that I need to mention here is that checking types in Tensorflow code is not easy. Without getting too deep into that, you can't simply define the type of x as a `tf.Tensor`. Type checking is great for simpler functions and basic data types but when it comes to Tensorflow code things can be hard. Pytype has the ability to infer some types from your code and it can resolve types such as Tensor or Module, but it doesn't always work as expected.

Linting tools such as Pylint can also be great for finding type errors from our IDE. **Linting** is the automated checking of your source code for programmatic and stylistic errors. This is done using a lint tool (otherwise known as linter) and the output is usually displayed inside the code editor or in the terminal.

4.1.5 Documentation

Documenting our code is the single most important thing in this list and the thing that most of us are guilty of not doing. Writing simple comments on our code can make the life of our teammates but also of our future selves much easier. It is even more important when we write deep learning code because of the complex nature of our software. In the same sense, it's equally important to give proper and descriptive names in our classes, functions and variables. Take a look at this:

```
def n(self, ii, im):
    ii = tf.cast(ii, tf.float32) / 255.0
    im -= 1
    return ii, im
```

I'm 100% certain that you have no idea what it does.

Now look at this:

```
def _normalize(self, input_image, input_mask):
        """ Normalise input image
        Args:
            input_image (tf.image): The input image
            input_mask (int): The image mask

        Returns:
            input_image (tf.image): The normalized input image
            input_mask (int): The new image mask
        """

        input_image = tf.cast(input_image, tf.float32) / 255.0
        input_mask -= 1
        return input_image, input_mask
```

Can it be more descriptive?

The comments you can see above are called **docstrings** and are Python's way to document the responsibility of a piece of code. I usually include a docstring at the beginning of a module (python file), indicating the purpose of a file, under every class declaration, and inside every function.

There are many ways to format the docstrings. I personally prefer the google style, which looks like the above code.

The first line always indicates what the code does, and it is the only real essential part. I personally try to always include this in my code. The other parts explain what arguments the function accepts (with types and descriptions) and what it returns. These can sometimes be ignored if they don't provide much value. Note that types provided in docstrings are different from type hints and a linter won't usually flag them.

4.2 Unit testing

Programming a deep learning model is not easy. I'm not going to lie to you. However, testing one is even harder. That's why most of the TensorFlow and Pytorch code out there does not include unit tests. But when your code is going to live in a production environment, making sure that it actually does what is intended, should be a priority. After all, machine learning is not different from any other software.

In this section, we are going to focus on how to properly test machine learning code, analyse a collection of best practices when writing unit tests, and present a number of example cases where testing is almost a necessity. We will start on why we need them in our code, then we will do a quick catch up on the basics of testing in Python. Finally we will go over different practical real-life scenarios.

Why do we need unit testing?

When developing a neural network, most of us don't care about catching all possible exceptions, finding all corner cases, or debugging every single function. We just need to see our model fitting. And then we just need to increase its accuracy until it reaches an acceptable percentage. That's all good but what happens when the model will be deployed into a server and used in an actual public-facing application? Most likely it will crash because some users may be sending wrong data or because of a silent bug that messes up our data pre-processing pipeline. We might even discover that our model was in fact corrupted all this time.

This is where unit tests come into play. To prevent all these things before they even occur. Unit tests are tremendously useful because they:

1. Find software bugs early.
2. Debug our code.
3. Ensure that the code does what it's supposed to do.
4. Simplify the refactoring process.
5. Speed up the integration process.
6. Act as documentation.

Don't tell me that you don't want at least some of the above. Sure, testing can take up a lot of our precious time but it's 100% worth it.

But what exactly is a unit test?

4.2.1 Basics of unit testing

In simple terms, **a unit test is basically a function calling another function (or a unit) and checking if the values returned match the expected output**. Let's see an example using our UNet model to make it clearer.

We have this simple function in our data pipeline that normalizes an image by dividing all the pixels by 255.

```
def _normalize(self, input_image, input_mask):
        """ Normalise input image
        Args:
            input_image (tf.image): The input image
            input_mask (int): The image mask

        Returns:
            input_image (tf.image): The normalized input image
            input_mask (int): The new image mask
        """

        input_image = tf.cast(input_image, tf.float32) / 255.0
        input_mask -= 1
        return input_image, input_mask
```

To make sure that it does exactly what it is supposed to do, we can write another function that uses `normalize()` and check its result. It will look something like this.

```
  def test_normalize(self):
        input_image = np.array([[1., 1.], [1., 1.]])
        input_mask = 1
        expected_image = np.array(
           [[0.00392157, 0.00392157], [0.00392157, 0.00392157]]
        )

        result = self.unet._normalize(input_image, input_mask)
        self.assertEquals(expected_image, result[0])
```

The `test_normalize()` function creates a fake input image, calls the function with that image as an argument, and then makes sure that the result is equal to the expected image. `assertEquals` is a special function, coming from the `unittest` package in Python and does exactly what its name suggests. It asserts that the two values are equal. Note that we can also use something like below, but using built-in functions has its advantages.

```
assert expected_image == result[0]
```

That's it. That's unit testing. Tests can be used on both very small functions and bigger, complicated functionalities across different modules. In the context of machine learning, we can test the deep learning models and all the surrounding components to make sure that the entire pipeline works as expected.

4.2.2 Unit tests in Python

Before we see more examples, I'd like to do a quick catch up on how Python supports unit testing.

The main testing framework/runner that comes into Python's standard library is `unittest`. `unittest` is pretty straightforward to use and it has only two requirements: to put your tests into a class and use its special assert functions. A simple example can be found below:

```
import unittest

class UnetTest(unittest.TestCase):

    def test_normalize(self):
        . . .

if __name__ == '__main__':
    unittest.main()
```

Some things to notice here:

1. We have our test class which includes a `test_normalize` function as a method. In general, test functions are named with `test_` as a prefix followed by the name of the function they test. (This is a convention, but it also enables `unittest`'s **autodiscovery** functionality, which is the ability of the library to automatically detect all unit tests within a project or a module. That way we won't have to run them one by one).

2. To run unit tests, we call the `unittest.main()` function which discovers all tests within the module, runs them and prints their output.

3. Our `UnetTest` class inherits the `unittest.TestCase` class. This class helps us set unique test cases with different inputs because it comes with `setUp()` and `tearDown()` methods. In `setUp()` we can define our inputs that can be accessed

by all tests, and in `tearDown()` we can dissolve them (see snippet in the next section). This is helpful because all tests should run independently and usually, they can't share information. Well, now they can.

Another two powerful frameworks are `pytest` and `nose`, which are pretty much governed by the same principles. I suggest playing with them a little before you decide what suits you best. I personally use `pytest` most of the times, because it feels a bit simpler and it supports a few nice to have things, like fixtures and test parameterization. But honestly, it doesn't have that big of a difference so you should be fine with either of them.

Sadly, unit testing in Tensorflow is not straightforward. For that reason, in the next section, I'm going to discuss another, lesser-known method.

4.2.3 Tests in Tensorflow

Since we use Tensorflow to program our model we can take advantage of `tf.test`, which is an extension of `unittest` but it contains assertions tailored to Tensorflow code. In that case, our code morphs into this:

```
import tensorflow as tf

class UnetTest(tf.test.TestCase):

    def setUp(self):
        super(UnetTest, self).setUp()
        ...

    def tearDown(self):
        pass

    def test_normalize(self):
        ...

if __name__ == '__main__':
    tf.test.main()
```

Did you notice anything familiar? Actually, it has exactly the same baselines with the caveat that we need to call the `super()` function inside `setup()`, which enables `tf.test` to do its magic. Pretty cool, right?

4.2.4 Mocking

Another super important topic we should be aware of is mocking and mock objects. Mocking classes and functions are common when writing Java but in Python they are underutilized. **Mocking makes it very easy to replace complex logic or heavy dependencies when testing code using dummy objects**. By dummy objects, we refer to simple, easy to code objects that have the same structure with our real objects but contain fake or useless data. In our image segmentation case, a dummy object might be a 4-dimensional tensor with all values equal to 1, which mimics an actual image.

Mocking also helps us control the code's behaviour and simulate expensive calls. Let's look at an example using once again our UNet model.

Let's assume that we want to make sure that the data pre-processing step is correct and that our code splits the data and creates the training and testing dataset as it should. This is a common real-life test case. Here is the code we want to test:

```
def load_data(self):
    """ Loads and Preprocess data """
    self.dataset, self.info =
    DataLoader().load_data(self.config.data)
    self.preprocess_data()

def _preprocess_data(self):
    """ Splits into training and test and set training parameters"""
    train = self.dataset['train'].map(
        self.load_image_train,
        num_parallel_calls = tf.data.experimental.AUTOTUNE
    )
    test = self.dataset['test'].map(self._load_image_test)

    self.train_dataset = train
        .cache()
        .shuffle(self.buffer_size)
        .batch(self.batch_size)
        .repeat()

    self.train_dataset = self.train_dataset.prefetch(
        buffer_size=tf.data.experimental.AUTOTUNE
    )
    self.test_dataset = test.batch(self.batch_size)
```

```python
def _load_image_train(self, datapoint):
    """ Loads and preprocess  a single training image """
    input_image = tf.image.resize(
        datapoint['image'], (self.image_size, self.image_size)
    )
    input_mask = tf.image.resize(
        datapoint['segmentation_mask'],
        (self.image_size, self.image_size)
    )

    if tf.random.uniform(()) > 0.5:
        input_image = tf.image.flip_left_right(input_image)
        input_mask = tf.image.flip_left_right(input_mask)

    input_image, input_mask = self._normalize(
        input_image, input_mask
    )

    return input_image, input_mask

def _load_image_test(self, datapoint):
    """ Loads and preprocess a single test image"""

    input_image = tf.image.resize(
        datapoint['image'], (self.image_size, self.image_size)
    )
    input_mask = tf.image.resize(
        datapoint['segmentation_mask'],
        (self.image_size, self.image_size)
    )

    input_image, input_mask = self._normalize(
        input_image, input_mask
    )

    return input_image, input_mask
```

This code actually handles the splitting, shuffling, resizing, batching (grouping) of the data. We will analyze it more extensively on Chapter 5. For now, suppose we want to test this code. Everything is nice and well **except the loading function**.

```
self.dataset, self.info = DataLoader().load_data(self.config.data)
```

Are we supposed to load the entire dataset every time we run a single unit test? Absolutely not. To avoid doing that, we could mock that function to return a dummy dataset instead of calling the real one. Mocking to the rescue.

We can do that with `unittests`'s mock object package. It provides a mock class `Mock()` to create a mock object directly and a `patch()` decorator. The decorator replaces an imported module, within the module we test, with a mock object. Ok, so how do we do that?

For those who aren't familiar, the **decorator** is simply a function that wraps another function to extend its functionality.

Once we declare the wrapper function, we can annotate other functions to enhance them. See the `@patch` below? That's a decorator which wraps the `test_load_data()` with the `patch()` function.

By using the `patch()` decorator we get this:

```
@patch('model.unet.DataLoader.load_data')
def test_load_data(self, mock_data_loader):

    mock_data_loader.side_effect = dummy_load_data
    shape = tf.TensorShape(
      [None, self.unet.image_size, self.unet.image_size, 3]
    )

    self.unet.load_data()
    mock_data_loader.assert_called()

    self.assertItemsEqual(
       self.unet.train_dataset.element_spec[0].shape, shape
    )
    self.assertItemsEqual(
       self.unet.test_dataset.element_spec[0].shape, shape
   )
```

What the decorator alongside the `mock_data_loader.side_effect = ...` does, is that the `DataLoader.load_data()` is "patched" by our `dummy_load_data()` function which returns a dummy dataset.

To sum up, instead of calling the actual function, we trigger the dummy function and we save ourselves from waiting for the dataset to be loaded in every single test. Plus, we get to control exactly what our input data should look like.

We can use a handy feature from the `tensorflow_datasets` package to build a mock dataset. This will return a mock dataset instead of the real one. Then we end up having a mock dataset object inside of a mock `load_data()` function. Inception. Or maybe Mockception!

```
import tensorflow_datasets as tfds

def dummy_load_data(*args, **kwargs):
    with tfds.testing.mock_data(num_examples=1):
        return tfds.load(CFG['data']['path'], with_info=True)
```

Remember, `CFG` refers to our configuration. I can tell that you are amazed by this. Don't try to hide it.

If you're still unclear with what we gained here, let me break it down. We managed to create a dummy object that mimics our entire dataset with a few lines of code. This object can now be used in different unit tests where the actual data are irrelevant to the functionality. We eliminated the need to load our actual dataset into memory just to perform a test.

One last thing we should mention is test coverage.

4.2.5 Test coverage

Before we see some specific testing use cases on machine learning, I would like to mention another important aspect. Coverage. By coverage, we mean how much of our code is actually tested by unit tests.

Coverage is an invaluable metric that can help us write better unit tests, discover which areas our tests don't exercise, find new test cases, and ensure the quality of our tests. We can simply check our test coverage following the steps below:

1) Install the coverage package

```
$ conda install coverage
```

2) Run the package in our test file

```
$ coverage run -m unittest
/home/aisummer/PycharmProjects/Deep-Learning-Production-Course/
model/tests/unet_test.py
```

3) Print the results

```
$ coverage report -m
/home/aisummer/PycharmProjects/Deep-Learning-Production-Course/model/
tests/unet_test.py

Name                          Stmts   Miss  Cover   Missing
---------------------------------------------------------------
model/tests/unet_test.py        35      1     97%     52
```

This says that we cover 97% of our code. There are 35 statements in total and we missed just 1 of them. The missing info tells us which lines of code still need coverage. In this way, you can keep track of the percentage of the tested code during your project development.

4.2.6 Test example cases

I think it's time to explore some of the different deep learning scenarios and parts of the codebase where unit testing can be incredibly useful. Well, I'm not going to write the code for every single one of them, but I think it would be very important to outline a few use cases.

We already discussed one of them. Ensuring that our data has the right format is critical. A few others I can think of are:

Data:

- Ensure that our data has the right format (yes, I put it again here for completion).
- Ensure that the training labels are correct.
- Test our complex processing steps such as image manipulation.
- Assert data completion, quality, and errors.
- Test the distribution of the features.

Training:

- Run a training step and compare the weights before and after, to ensure that they are updated.
- Check that our loss function can be actually used on our data.

Evaluation:

- Having tests to ensure that your metrics (e.g. accuracy, precision, and recall) are above a threshold when iterating over different architectures.
- We can run speed/benchmark tests on training to catch possible overfitting.
- Of course, cross-validation can be in the form of a unit test.

Model Architecture:

- The model's layers are stacking.
- The model's output has the correct shape.

On second thought, let's program the last one to prove to you how simple it is:

```
def test_ouput_size(self):
    shape = (1, self.unet.image_size, self.unet.image_size, 3)
    image = tf.ones(shape)
    self.unet.build()
    self.assertEqual(self.unet.model.predict(image).shape, shape)
```

That's it. Define the expected shape, construct a dummy input, build the model, and run a prediction is all it takes. Not so bad for such a useful test, right? You see unit tests don't have to be complex. **Sometimes a few lines of code can save us from a lot of trouble**. Trust me. At the same time though, we shouldn't go on the other side and test every single thing imaginable. This is a huge time sink. As always, we need to find a balance.

I am confident that you can come up with many more test scenarios when developing your own models. Now that you have a rough but clear idea what tests are, you can find the ones that suit best to your work.

4.2.7 Integration / acceptance tests

Something that I deliberately avoided mentioning is **Integration and Acceptance Tests (ATs)** . These kinds of tests are very powerful tools and **aim to test how well our system integrates with other systems**. If you have an application with many services or a client/server interaction, acceptance tests are the go-to functionality to make sure that everything works as expected at a higher level.

Later throughout the book, when we deploy our model in a server, we will need to write some acceptance tests as we want to be certain that the model returns what the user/client expects in the form that they expect it. As we iterate over our application while it is live and is served to users, we can't have a failure due to a minor bug. These are the kinds of things that acceptance tests help us avoid.

Unfortunately, you will have to wait for the last chapters to see how we can build an acceptance test. It's quite straightforward and has the form of a unit test, but it requires us to have two separate systems. In our example, we will use a server containing our model and a client. More on that in Chapter 7.

4.3 Debugging

Have you ever been stuck on an error for way too long? I remember once when I spent over 2 weeks on a small typo that didn't crash the program but returned inexplicable results. I literally couldn't sleep because of this. I'm 100% certain that this has happened to you as well, therefore now we will be focusing on how to debug deep learning code and how to use logging to catch bugs. We will of course use Tensorflow to showcase some examples, following our image segmentation project, but the exact same principles apply to Pytorch or other AI frameworks.

As I said at the beginning of the book, **machine learning is ordinary software and should always be treated like one**. And one of the most essential parts of the software development lifecycle is debugging. Proper debugging can help eliminate future pains when our algorithms are been used by real users. It can make our system as robust and reliable as our users expect it to be.

4.3.1 How to a debug deep learning project?

Deep learning debugging is more difficult than normal software because of multiple reasons:

- Poor model performance does not imply bugs in the code.
- The iteration cycle (building the model, training, and testing) is quite long.
- Training/testing data can also have errors and anomalies.
- Hyperparameters affect the final accuracy.
- It's not always deterministic (e.g. probabilistic machine learning).
- Static computation graphs (e.g. Tensorflow 1.0 and CNTK) prevent line by line execution of the code.

Based on the above, the best way to start thinking about debugging is to **simplify the ML model development process as much as possible**. By simplifying, I mean to a ridiculous level. In general, when experimenting with our model, the best practice is to start from a simple algorithm. It is also common to utilize only a handful of features and gradually keep expanding by adding features and tuning hyperparameters while keeping the model simple. Once we find a satisfactory set of features, we can start increasing our model's complexity, keep track of the metrics, and continue incrementally until the results are satisfactory for our application.

In the image segmentation case, we don't really have a choice but to use the image. We can however start with a simple U-shaped convolutional network. There are tons of variations of Unet for image segmentation, but the standard baseline will work just fine as a first step. Furthermore, research papers are too much focused on the modelling part for fixed datasets. This is rarely helpful in a production environment. Now we will mostly care about our data and our model lifecycle.

But even in these case, bugs and anomalies might occur. In fact, they will definitely occur. When they do, our next step is to take advantage of Python's debugging capabilities.

4.3.2 Python's debugger

Python debugger (Pdb) is part of the Python standard library. **The debugger is essentially a program that can monitor the state of our own program while it is running.** The most important command of any debugger is called a breakpoint. We can set a breakpoint anywhere in our code and the debugger will stop the execution at this exact point and give us access to the values of all the variables at that point, as well as the traceback of python calls.

There are two ways to interact with Python's debugger. Command line and IDEs. If you want to use the terminal you can go ahead, but I must warn you that it's quite tedious. You will have to insert the breakpoints inside the code and interact with the debugger through the terminal.

```
import pdb
pdb.set_trace()
```

Since we have used PyCharm throughout the book, we will stay consistent and use it here as well.

Let's have a closer look at the Figure 4.1. As you can see, we have set a breakpoint (the red dot on line 124) at the beginning of the for-loop in the `predict()` function, and we pressed the debug button.

The program then was executed normally until it hit the breakpoint where the debugger paused the state. In the debug window below the code, we can inspect all the variables at this stage of the execution. Let's assume for example that we wanted to debug the size of the input image: as you can see it's 128. Or the number of epoches. Again, it's very easy to spot that it's 20.

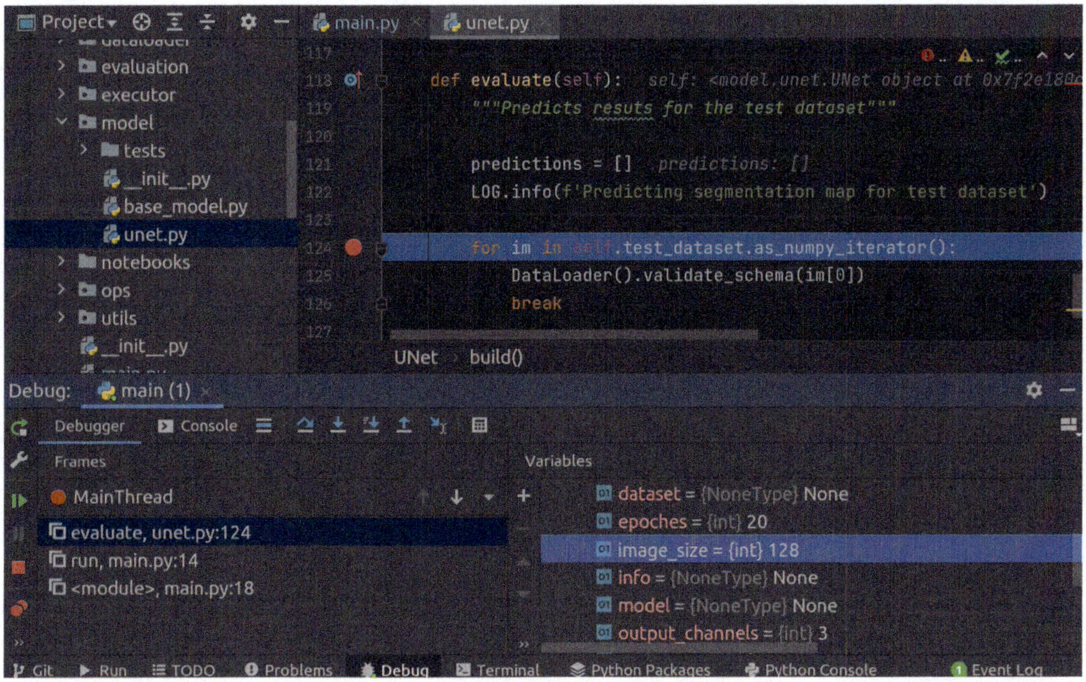

Figure 4.1: Python debugging on Pycharm

Tip: Using the debugger, we can access anywhere, any variable we want. Therefore, we can avoid having print statements all over the place.

From the breakpoint, we can continue to another breakpoint, or we can finish the program's execution. We also have a 3rd option. We can use the step function of the debugger to go into the next code line. And then go to the second next line. That way, we can choose to run our code as slowly as we want until we figure out what is wrong.

4.3.3 Debugging data with schema validation

Now that we have a decent way to find bugs in the code, we should have a look at the second most common source of errors in machine learning: data. As you can imagine, data aren't always in perfect form. And in fact they never are in real-life scenarios. Let me give you an example: they may contain corrupted data points, some values may be missing, they may have a different format. They may even have a different range/distribution than expected.

To catch all these before training or prediction, one of the most common ways is **Schema Validation**. We can define the **schema as a contract of the format of**

our data. Practically, the schema is a file containing all the required features for a model, their form and their type. Note that it can be in whichever format we want (many Tensorflow models use proto files). To monitor the incoming data and catch abnormalities, we can validate them against the schema. This will help us automate the data checking process.

Schema validation is especially useful when the model is deployed on a production environment and accepts user generated data. In the case of our project, once we have the UNet running in production, the user will be able to send any image he wants. As a result, we need to have a way to validate them before feeding them into the model.

Since our input data are images, which are literally 4-dimensional tensors of shape [batch, channels, height, width], an example schema will look as depicted below. Note that this is not what your typical schema will look like. Since we deal with images as inputs, we should be concise and give the correct schema as illustrated below:

```
SCHEMA = {
  "type": "object",
  "properties": {
    "image":{
        "type":"array",
        "items":{
            "type": "array",
            "items": {
                "type": "array",
                "items": {
                    "type": "array",
                    "items": {
                        "type": "number"
                    }
                }
            }
        }
    }
  },
  "required":["image"]
}
```

Essentially, our data type is a Python object as you can see in the first line. This object contains a property called `image` which is of type `array` and has a set of items. Typically, your schema will end at this point, but in our case, we need to go deep to declare all 4 dimensions of our image.

You can think of it as a type of recursion where we define the same item inside the other. Deep into the recursion, we define the type of our values to be numeric. Finally, the last line of the schema indicates all the required properties of our object. In this particular case, it's just the image.

A more common example of what a schema will look is the below:

```
SCHEMA = {
  "type": "object",
  "properties":{
    "feature-1":{
        "type":"string"
      },
    "feature-2":{
        "type":"integer"
     },
    "feature-3":{
        "type":"string"
    }
  },
  "required":["feature-1", "feature-3"]
}
```

In that case, we should expect data such as the one below:

```
{
  "feature-1": "deep-learning",
  "feature-2" : 45,
  "feature-3": "production"
}
```

I hope that clears things up. Once we have our schema, we can use it to validate our data. In Python, there is the built-in `jsonschema` package, which can help us do exactly that.

```
import jsonschema
from configs.data_schema import SCHEMA



class DataLoader:
    """Data Loader class"""
```

```
    @staticmethod
    def validate_schema(data_point):
        jsonschema.validate({'image':data_point.tolist()}, SCHEMA)
```

We can call the `validate_schema()` function whenever we like to check our data against our schema. How does it compare to running `print(tensor.shape)` everywhere around your production codebase? More elegant and easy, I would dare to say.

Caveat: Schema validation is an expensive and very slow operation in general, so we should think carefully where and when to enforce it because it will affect our program performance.

Advanced Tip: For those who use Tensorflow Extended (TFX) to serve their models, the data validation library can infer a schema automatically from the data. More on that on Chapter 10.

4.3.4 Logging

Logging goes hand in hand with debugging. Logs are records relevant to our software that are printed or stored. Logging is the act of keeping a log. But why do we need to keep logs? Logs are an essential part of troubleshooting applications and infrastructure performance. When our code is executed on a production environment in a remote machine, for instance Google Cloud, we can't really go there and start printing stuff around. Instead, in such remote environments, we use logs to have a clear image of what's going on. Logs do not exist only to capture the state of our program but also to discover possible exceptions and errors.

But why not use simple print statements? Aren't they enough? Actually, no they are not! Why? Here is an outline of some advantages logs provide over print statements:

- **We can log different severity levels** (DEBUG, INFO, WARNING, ERROR, CRITICAL) and choose to show only the level we care about. For example, we can stuff our code with debug logs, but we may not want to show all of them in production to avoid having millions of log rows. Instead, we show only warnings and errors.
- **We can choose the output channel**. This is not possible with prints as they always use the console. Some of our options are writing them to a file, sending them over http, printing them on the console, streaming them to a secondary location, or even sending them over email.

- **Timestamps are included by default.**
- The format of the message is easily **configurable.**

Tip: A general rule of thumb is to avoid print statements as much as possible and replace them with either debugging processes or logs.

And it's incredibly easy to use. Let's dive in and use it in our codebase.

4.3.5 Python's Logging module

Python's default module for logging is called `logging`. In order to use it, all we have to do is:

```
import logging

logging.warning('Warning. Our pants are on fire...")
```

But since we are developing a production-ready pipeline with highly extensible and modularized code, we should include it in a more elegant way. We can go into the `utils` folder and create a file called `logger.py` so we can import it anywhere we like.

```
import logging.config
import yaml

with open('configs/logging_config.yaml', 'r') as f:
    config = yaml.safe_load(f.read())
    logging.config.dictConfig(config)
    logging.captureWarnings(True)

def get_logger(name: str):
    """Logs a message
    Args:
    name(str): name of logger
    """
    logger = logging.getLogger(name)
    return logger
```

The `get_logger` function will be imported when we want to log stuff and it will create a logger with a specific name. The `name` is essential so we can identify the origin of our log rows. To make the logger easily configurable, we will put all the specifications inside a config file. And since we already saw json formats, let's use a different format called `yaml`. In practice it's better to stick with a single format but here I will use a different one for educational purposes.

Our file will load the yaml file and will pass its parameters into the `logging module` to set its default behaviour.

A simple configuration file looks something like this:

```
version: 1
formatters:
  simple:
    format: '%(asctime)s - %(name)s - %(levelname)s - %(message)s'
handlers:
  console:
    class: logging.StreamHandler
    formatter: simple
    stream: ext://sys.stdout
Root:
  Level: DEBUG
  handlers: [console]
```

As you can see:

- We set the default format in the `formatters` node.
- We define the console as the output channel (`handler`) and streaming as the transmission method.
- We set the default level to `DEBUG`. This means that all logs above that level will be printed.

Important information: For reference, the order of levels is: DEBUG < INFO < WARNING < ERROR < CRITICAL.

So whenever we need to log something, all we have to do is import the file and use the built-in functions such as `.info()`, `.debug()` and `.error()`.

```
from utils.logger import get_logger

LOG = get_logger('unet')

def evaluate(self):
    """Predicts results for the test dataset"""

    predictions = []
```

```
    LOG.info('Predicting segmentation map for test dataset')

    for image, mask in self.test_dataset:
        LOG.debug(f'Predicting segmentation map {image}')
        predictions.append(self.model.predict(image))
    return predictions
```

A good practice is to log `info` on critical turning points such as "Data loading", "Data pre-processed", "Training started" and use `debug` to print data points, variables, tensor shapes. and lower-level details.

Tip: In general, most engineers log info and above levels, when the code is executed in a production environment and keep the debug level for when things break in order to debug a functionality.

Last but not least, I want to close this chapter by mentioning a few extremely useful Tensorflow functions and packages we can use to log Tensorflow-related stuff.

4.3.6 Useful Tensorflow debugging and logging functions

I feel like I should warn you that in this section, we will take a rather deep dive into Tensorflow so if you are not familiar with it or you prefer a different framework feel free to skip. But since our codebase for this book is using Tensorflow, I couldn't really avoid mentioning these.

Let's start with the definition of the computational graph because it is directly important on how logging works on Tensorflow.

A computational graph is defined as a directed graph where the nodes correspond to mathematical operations. Computational graphs are a way of expressing and evaluating a mathematical expression. Most deep learning frameworks define a computational graph each time a model is compiled. That way backpropagation can easily be executed regardless of the complexity of the model architecture. In more details, the framework applies recursively the chain rule to compute the gradients all the way to the inputs of the graph.

Tensorflow code is not your normal code and as we said before, it's not trivial to debug and test it. One of the main reasons is that Tensorflow used to have a static computational graph, meaning that you had to define the model, compile it and then run it. This made debugging much, much harder, because we couldn't access variables and states as we normally do in other applications.

However, in Tensorflow 2.0 the default execution mode is the eager (dynamic) mode, meaning that the graph is dynamic following the Pytorch pattern. Of course, there

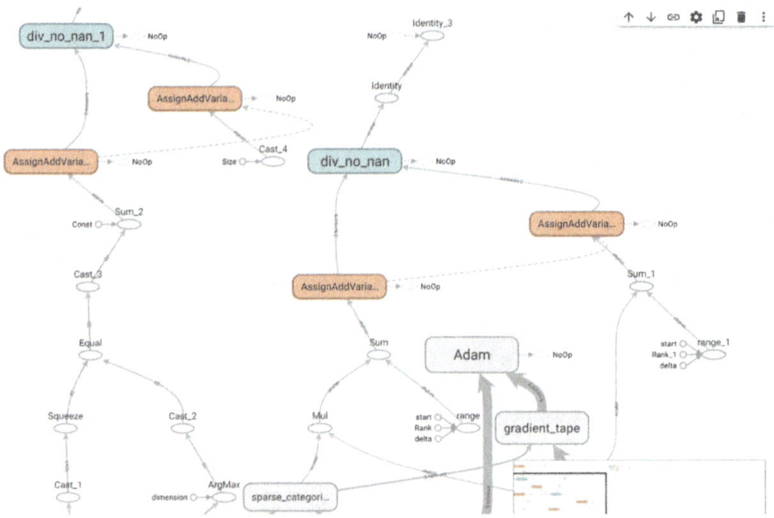

Figure 4.2: A computational graph

are still cases when the code can't be executed eagerly. And even in eager mode, the computational graph still exists in the background. That's why we need these functions as they have been built with that in mind. They provide additional flexibility that normal logging simply won't.

Note: The Python debugger works only when Tensorflow is running in eager mode because the graph is compiled.

1. `tf.print` is Tensorflow's built-in print function that can be used to print tensors but also to let us define the output stream and the current level. It is based on the fact that it is actually a separate component inside the computational graph. Thus, it communicates by default with all the other components. Especially in the case that a function is not run eagerly, normal print statements won't work and we have to use `tf.print()`.

2. `tf.Variable.assign` can be used to assign values to a variable during runtime, in case you want to test things or explore different alternatives. It will directly change the computational graph so that the new value can be picked from the rest of the nodes.

3. `tf.summary` provides an API to write summary data into files. Let's say we want to save metrics on a file or a specific tensor to track its values. We can do just that with `tf.summary()`. In essence, it's a logging system to save anything we like into a file. Plus, it is integrated with Tensorboard so we can visualize our summaries with little effort.

4. `tf.debugging` is a set of assert functions (tailored to tensors) that can be put inside our code to validate our data, our weights or our model.
5. `tf.debugging.enable_metrics()` is part of the same module but I had to mention it separately because it's simply amazing. This little function will cause the code to error out as soon as an operation's output tensor contains infinity or NaN. This is really helpful in a production environment as well as during training.
6. `get_concrete_function(input).graph`. This simple but amazing function can be used to convert any python function into a `tf.Graph` so we can access all sorts of things from here (shapes, value types etc).
7. `tf.keras.callbacks` are functions that are used during training to pass information to external sources. The most common use case is passing training data into Tensorboard but that is not all. They can also be used to save csv data, early stop the training based on a metric, or even change the learning rate. It's an extremely useful tool especially for those who don't want to write Tensorflow code and prefer the simplicity of Keras.

Here is an example on how to use Tensorboard with a simple callback:

```
model.fit(
    x_train, # input
    y_train, # output
    batch_size=train_size,
    verbose=0, # Suppress chatty output; use Tensorboard instead
    epochs=100,
    validation_data=(x_test, y_test),
    callbacks=[tf.keras.callbacks.TensorBoard(log_dir=logdir)],
)
```

You will find more details about Tensorboard on the section 6.1.4.

Chapter 5

Data Processing

In this chapter:

- How to build a data pipeline
- What are the steps of data pre-processing
- How to optimize a data pipeline

It's time to explore big data processing. Building an efficient data pipeline is an essential part of developing an AI product and something that should not be taken lightly. As I'm pretty sure you know by now, machine learning is completely useless without curated data. Curated data is data from the correct sources and in the proper format.

But what is a data pipeline? And when do we characterize it as efficient?

Generally speaking, data prepossessing consists of two steps: **data engineering and feature engineering**.

- Data engineering is the process of converting raw data into prepared data, which can be used for ML.
- Feature engineering extracts informative features that we expect to give us a good performance.

When we deal with a small amount of data, building a pipeline is usually straightforward. But that's almost never the case with deep learning. Here we play with very large datasets. Think of the sizes in GBs or even TBs in some cases. Manipulating those amounts is definitely not a piece of cake. But dealing with difficult software challenges is what this book is all about.

Let's start with the fundamentals.

5.1 ETL: Extract, Transform, Load

In the wonderful world of databases, there is this notion called ETL. As you can see in the headline, ETL is an acronym of Extract, Transform, Load. These are the 3 building blocks of most data pipelines.

- **Extraction** involves the process of extracting the data from multiple homogeneous or heterogeneous sources.
- **Transformation** refers to data cleansing and manipulation in order to convert them into a proper format.
- **Loading** is the injection of the transformed data into the memory of the processing units that will handle the training, whether these are CPUs, GPUs or even TPUs.

When we combine these 3 steps, we get the notorious data pipeline. However, there is a caveat here. It's not enough to build an ETL pipeline. It's equally important to make it fast. Speed and performance are key parts of building a data pipeline. Let's analyse why.

Imagine that each training epoch of our model is taking 10 minutes to complete. What happens if the ETL of the segment of the required data can't be finished in less than 15 minutes? The training will remain idle for 5 minutes. You may say fine, it's offline, who cares? But when the model goes online, what happens if the processing of a single image takes 2 minutes? The user will have to wait for 2 minutes plus the inference time. Let me tell you that 2 minutes in browser response time is simply unacceptable for good user experience.

Let's see how things work in practice. Before we dive into the details, we will explore some of the problems we want to address when constructing an input pipeline. Because it's not just speed, if only it was. We also care about **throughput, latency, ease of implementation and maintenance**. In more details, we might need to solve problems such as:

- Data might not fit into memory.
- Data might not even fit into the local storage.
- Data might come from multiple sources.

- Utilize hardware as efficiently as possible both in terms of resources and idle time.
- Make processing fast so it can keep up with the accelerator's speed.
- The result of the pipeline should often be deterministic.
- Being able to define our own specific transformations.
- Being able to visualize the process.

These are the core axons that you have to consider when designing your production ETL pipeline. I will try to unravel these considerations one by one. For each part of the pipeline, I will first highlight the core concepts and the problem we address. Then I will present a few lines of code. Yes, thanks to Tensorflow and the `tf.data` module, input pipelines are usually just a few lines of code. For our use case, we will use the pet images dataset from the Visual Geometry Group of Oxford University.

Figure 5.1: Pet images dataset from Oxford university

5.2 Data reading

Data reading or extracting is when we get the data from the data source and convert them, from the format they are stored, into our desired one. You may wonder where the difficulty lies. We can just run a `pandas.read_csv()`. Well not quite. In the modeling phase of machine learning, we are used to have all the data locally. However, in a production environment the data might be stored in a database, like MySQL or MongoDB. In bigger scales the data will be stored in a cloud storage service like AWS S3 or Google Cloud storage, or even in a data warehouse (i.e. Amazon Redshift or Google BigQuery). And each storage option has its own set of rules on how to extract and parse data.

5.2.1 Loading from multiple sources

That's why we need to be able to consolidate and combine all these different sources into a single entity. The extracted data will be passed into the next step of the pipeline. Since each source has a specific format to store them, we need a way to decode them as well. Here is a boilerplate code that uses `tf.data`:

```
files = tf.data.Dataset.list_files(file_pattern)
dataset = tf.data.TFRecordDataset(files)
```

The `tf.data` package is the default data manipulation library of Tensorflow. Here, we define a list of files based on a pattern and then we construct a `TFRecordDataset` from those files. For example, in the case that our data are on AWS s3, we might have something like that:

```
filenames = ["s3://bucketname/path/to/file1.tfrecord",
             "s3://bucketname/path/to/file2.tfrecord"]
dataset = tf.data.TFRecordDataset(filenames)
```

In our case with the pet images, can we simply do this?

```
dataset = tf.data.TFRecordDataset(
http://www.robots.ox.ac.uk/~vgg/data/pets/data/images.tar.gz
)
```

Unfortunately, no. You see, the data should be in a format and in a source supported by Tensorflow. What we want to do here is to manually download, unzip and convert the raw images into `tf.Record` or another compatible with Tensorflow format. Luckily, there is another way. We can use the Tensorflow datasets library (`tf.tdfs`), which wraps all this functionality and returns a ready to use `tf.Dataset`.

```
import tensorflow_datasets as tfds

tfds.load("oxford_iiit_pet:3.*.*", with_info=True)
```

Or more precisely in our own code we have:

```
@staticmethod
def load_data(data_config):
    """Loads dataset from path"""
    return tfds.load(
        data_config.path, with_info=data_config.load_with_info
    )
```

The `info` will be provided from the config file, which makes things easily configurable. Nonetheless, for unsupported datasets, I'm afraid that we have to do that ourselves and create a custom data loader.

Tip: Good knowledge of our data source intricacies is almost always necessary for effective data loading.

By the way, there is an excellent library called **TensorFlow I/O** to help us deal with more data formats. It even supports DICOM, a medical image format.

Are you discouraged already? Don't be. Creating data loaders is an essential part of being a ML Engineer.

5.2.2 Parallel data extraction

In cases where our data are stored remotely, loading them can become a bottleneck in the pipeline. Why? Because it can significantly increase the latency and lower the throughput. **The time that takes for the data to be extracted from the source and transmitted into our system, is an important factor to take into consideration.** Let's find ways to tackle this bottleneck in action.

The answer that comes first to mind is **parallelization** . Since we haven't touched upon parallel processing so far in the book, let's give a quick definition:

Parallel processing is a type of computation in which many calculations or the execution of processes are carried out simultaneously.

Modern computing systems include multiple CPU cores, so why not take advantage of all of them? Always remember the efficient hardware utilization principle. For example, my laptop has 8 cores. Wouldn't it be reasonable to assign each core to a different batch and load eight of them in RAM or VRAM at the same time? Luckily, it is as easy as this:

```
tf.data.Dataset.list_files(file_pattern)
tf.data.interleave(TFRecordDataset, num_calls=8)
```

The `interleave()` function will load many batches concurrently and interleave the results in 8 processes so we don't have to wait for each one of them to be loaded.

Before the introduction of parallelization, the processing flow for the extraction was something like this:

```
Open connection ->  read batch 1 -> continue -> read batch 2
-> continue
```

But now it is something like this

```
Open connection -> read batch 1 -> continue ->
                -> read batch 2 -> continue ->
                -> read batch 3 -> continue ->
                -> read batch 4 -> continue ->
```

5.3 Processing

We loaded our data in parallel from all the sources, and now we are ready to apply transformations to them. In this step, **we are running the most computationally intense functions** such as image manipulation, data decoding and literally anything you can code. In the image segmentation example, this will be resizing our images, flip a portion of them horizontally to introduce variance in our dataset, and finally normalize them. Although, let me introduce another new concept before that.

Functional programming is a programming paradigm in which we build software by stacking pure functions, avoiding sharing state between them, and using immutable data. In functional programming, the logic and data flow through functions, inspired by mathematics.

Does that make sense? I'm sure it doesn't. Let's give an example.

```
import pandas as pd

df = read.csv("titanic_dataset.csv")
df.rename(columns={"titanic_survivors": "survivors"})
  .query("survivors_age > 14 and survivors_gender == 'female'")
  .sort_values("survivors_age", ascending=False)
```

Does that seem familiar? It's pure pandas code. Notice how we chained the methods so that **each function is called after the previous one**. Also notice that we don't share information between functions and that the original dataset flows throughout the chain. That way we don't need to have for-loops, reassign variables, or create a new dataframe every time we apply a new transformation. Plus, it is very easy to parallelize this code.

How? Remember the trick above in the interleave function where we add a `num_calls` argument? Well, the reason we were able to do that so effortlessly is functional programming.

But why do we care? Functional programming supports many different functions such as `filter()`, `sort()` and more. But the most important one is called `map()`. With map() we can apply almost any function we may think of.

Note that map() is a special function that applies another function to each element of a collection. Instead of writing a for-loop and iterating over all elements, we can map all the collection's elements to the result of the user-defined function. And of course, it follows the functional paradigm. Actually, let's look at a simple example to make that crystal clear.

Imagine that we have a list [1,2,3,4] and we want to add 1 to each element and produce a new array with values [2,3,4,5]. In normal Python code we have:

```
m_list = [1,2,3,4]
for i in m_list:
    m[i] = m[i] +1
```

But in functional programming we can do:

```
m_list = list( map( lambda i: i+1, m_list) )
```

And the result is the same. What's the advantage?

- It's much simpler.
- It improves maintainability.
- We can define extremely complex functions easily.
- It provides modularity.
- It is shorter.

Plus, it makes parallelization so much easier. Try to parallelize the above for-loop. Seriously, I dare you.

In the segmentation example, we can do something similar. So far, we have a preprocessing function that resizes, randomly flips, and normalizes the images.

```
@staticmethod
def _preprocess_train(datapoint, image_size):
    """ Loads and preprocess  a single training image """
    input_image = tf.image.resize(
       datapoint['image'], (image_size, image_size)
    )
    input_mask = tf.image.resize(
       datapoint['segmentation_mask'], (image_size, image_size)
    )
```

```
    if tf.random.uniform(()) > 0.5:
        input_image = tf.image.flip_left_right(input_image)
        input_mask = tf.image.flip_left_right(input_mask)

    input_image, input_mask = DataLoader.normalize(
       input_image, input_mask
    )
    return input_image, input_mask
```

We can now add the pre-processing step to the data pipeline using `map()` and lambda functions. The result is:

```
@staticmethod
def preprocess_data(dataset, batch_size, buffer_size,image_size):
    """ Preprocess and splits into training and test"""
    train = dataset['train'].map(
       lambda image: DataLoader.preprocess_train(
            image,image_size
       ), num_parallel_calls = tf.data.experimental.AUTOTUNE
    )
    train_dataset = train.shuffle(buffer_size)

    test = dataset['test'].map(
        lambda image: DataLoader._preprocess_test(image, image_size)
    )
    test_dataset = test.shuffle(buffer_size)

    return train_dataset, test_dataset
```

As you can see, we have two different pipelines. One for the training dataset and one for the test dataset. See how we first apply the `map()` function and sequentially the `shuffle()`? The `map` function will apply the `_preprocess_train()` in every single data instance. And once the pre-processing is finished, it will shuffle the dataset.

That's functional programming. **No share of objects between functions, no mutability of objects, no unnecessary side effects**. We just declare our desired functionality and that's it.

Notice also the `num_parallel_calls` argument. Yes, we will run the function in parallel. And thanks to Tensorflow's built-in autotuning, we don't even have to worry about setting the number of calls. It will figure it out by itself, based on our environment and hardware. How cool is that?

Finally, on our image segmentation example, the whole pipeline looks like this:

```
def load_data(self):
    """Loads and Preprocess data """
    LOG.info(f'Loading {self.config.data.path} dataset...')
    self.dataset, self.info =
        DataLoader().load_data(self.config.data)
    self.train_dataset, self.test_dataset =
        DataLoader.preprocess_data(
            self.dataset, self.batch_size,
            self.buffer_size, self.image_size
        )
    self._set_training_parameters()
```

Not that bad, right?

Besides `map()`, `tf.data` also supports many other useful functions such as:

- `filter()`: filters dataset based on condition
- `shuffle()`: randomly shuffles dataset
- `skip()`: removes elements from the pipeline
- `concatenate()`: combines 2 or more datasets
- `cardinality()`: returns the number of elements in the dataset

Keep these functions in the back of your mind. They may be proved useful in your future projects. Furthermore, it contains some extremely powerful functions like `batch()`, `prefetch()`, `cache()`, `reduce()`, which are the topic of a following section.

5.4 Loading

Loading essentially refers to passing the data into our model for training. In terms of the code is as simple as writing:

```
self.model.fit(
    self.train_dataset,
    epochs=self.epoches,
    steps_per_epoch=self.steps_per_epoch,
    validation_steps=self.validation_steps,
```

```
    validation_data=self.test_dataset
)
```

All we did here, was call the `fit()` function of the Keras API, define the number of epochs, the number of steps per epoch, the validation steps, and simply pass the data as an argument. Is that enough? If only it was that easy.

Actually, let's remember our current pipeline until now.

```
self.dataset, self.info = DataLoader().load_data(self.config.data)
train = self.dataset['train'].map(
    lambda image: DataLoader.preprocess_train(image,image_size),
    num_parallel_calls=tf.data.experimental.AUTOTUNE
)
train_dataset = train.shuffle(buffer_size)
```

Recap: We are loading our data using the Tensorflow dataset library, we then use the `map()` function to apply some sort of pre-processing into each data instance, and then we shuffle them. The pre-processing function resizes each data instance, flips it, and normalizes the image.

So you might think that, since the images are extracted from the data source and transformed into the right format, we can just go ahead and pass them into the `fit()` function. In theory, yes, this is correct. However, in practice we don't just want to pass the data into a `fit()` function. We may care about having more explicit control of the training loop. To this end, we need to iterate over the data, which translates to constructing the training loop as we'd like.

Tip: Running a for-loop in a dataset is almost always a bad idea because it will load the entire dataset into memory. Instead, we want to use Python's iterators.

5.4.1 Iterators

An iterator is nothing more than an object that enables us to traverse throughout our collection, usually a list. In our case, that collection is a dataset. The big advantage of iterators is lazy loading. Instead of loading the entire dataset into memory, the iterator loads each data instance only when it is needed. Needless to say that this is what `tf.data` is using behind the scenes. But we can also do that manually.

In `tf.data` code we can have something like this:

```
dataset = tf.data.Dataset.range(2)
for element in dataset:
```

```
  train(element)
```

Or we can simply get the iterator using the `iter` function and then loop over it using the `get_next` function:

```
iterator = iter(dataset)
train(iterator.get_next())
```

Or we can use Python's built-in `next` function:

```
iterator = iter(dataset)
train(next(iterator))
```

We can also get a Numpy iterator from a Tensorflow Dataset object:

```
for element in dataset.as_numpy_iterator():
  train(element)
```

We have many options, that's for sure. We also do care about performance.

Ok, I keep referencing performance, but I haven't really explained what that means. Performance in terms of what? How can we measure it? If I had to put it in a few words, I would say that **performance is how fast the whole pipeline from extraction to loading is executed**. If I wanted to dive a little deeper, I would say that performance is latency, throughput, ease of implementation, maintenance, and hardware utilization.

5.5 Optimizing a data pipeline

You see, getting the required data for training a deep neural network is not trivial. Sometimes we aren't able to load all of them into memory. Meanwhile, each processing step might take far too long to complete, and the model will have to wait until then. There are use cases where we don't have enough resources to manipulate all of them.

In the previous section, we discussed a well-known trick to address some of the issues, called parallel processing. Basically, we run the operation simultaneously into our different CPU cores. This time, we will focus on some other techniques. The first one is called batching.

5.5.1 Batching

Batch processing has a slightly different meaning between a software engineer and a machine learning engineer. The former thinks **batching as a method to run high volume, repetitive jobs into groups with no human interaction** while the latter thinks of it as the partitioning of data into chunks.

In software engineering, batching help us avoid having computer resources idle and run the jobs when the resources are available. In machine learning, batches make the training much more efficient because of the way the stochastic gradient descent algorithm works.

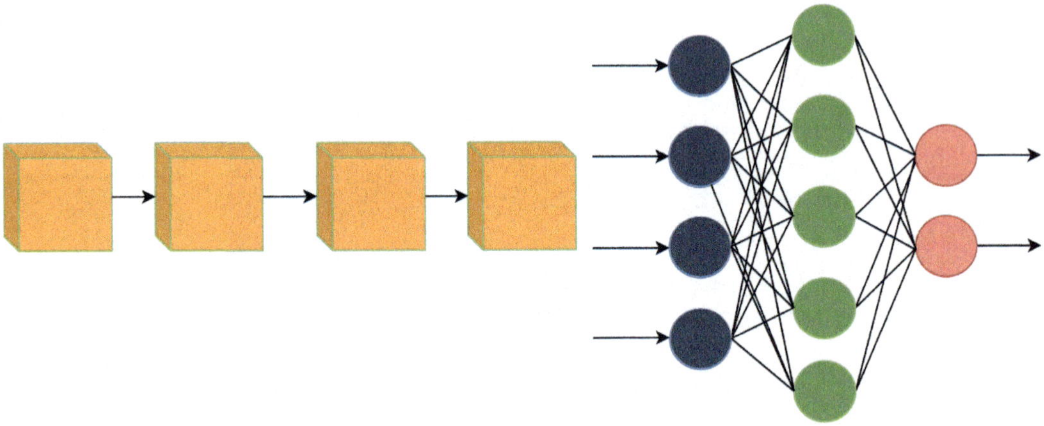

Figure 5.2: Batching

I'm not going to dive deep into many details, but in essence, instead of updating the weights after training on every single training example, we update them after every batch. This modification of the algorithm is called Batch Gradient Descent.

In Tensorflow, creating batches (data chunks) with `tf.data` is as easy as this:

```
train = train.batch(batch_size)
```

That way, after loading and manipulating our data, we can split them into small chunks in order to pass them into the model for training. Not only do we train our model using batch gradient descent, but also **we apply all of our transformations on one batch at a time, avoiding loading all our data into memory at once**. Please note that the batch size refers to the number of elements in each batch.

Now pay attention to this: we load a batch; we process it and then we feed it into the model for training in a sequential order. Does that mean that while the model is running, the whole pipeline remains idle waiting for the training to be completed?

That's right. Ideally, we would want to do both of these operations at the same time. While the model is training on a batch, we could process the next batch simultaneously.

Can we do that? Of course!

5.5.2 Prefetching

Tensorflow gives us the ability to prefetch the data while our model is training using the `prefetch` function. **Prefetching overlaps the pre-processing with the model execution of a training step**. While the model is executing training step "n", the input pipeline is reading the data for step "n+1". That way, we can reduce not only the overall processing time, but the training time as well.

```
train = train.prefetch(buffer_size=tf.data.experimental.AUTOTUNE)
```

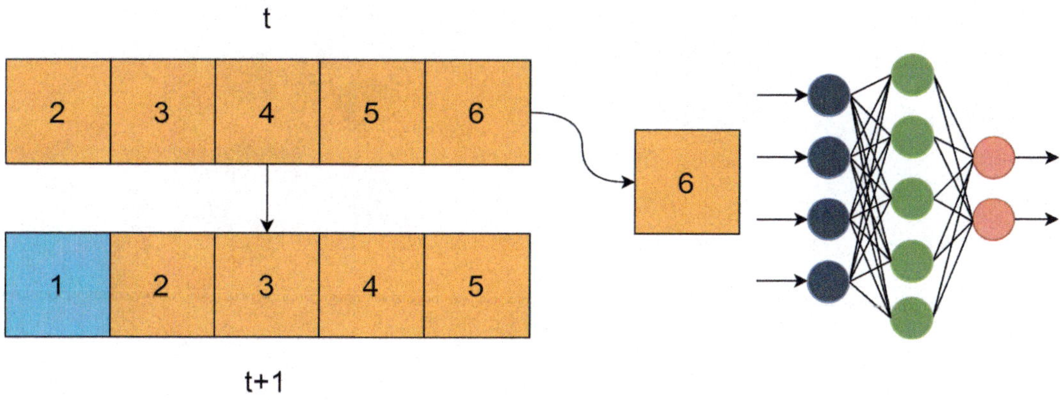

Figure 5.3: Prefetching

For those who are more tech-savvy, using prefetching is like having a decoupled producer-consumer system coordinated by a buffer. In our case, the producer is the data processing step and the consumer is the model. The buffer handles the transportation of the data from one to the other. Keep in mind that the buffer size should be equal or less than the number of elements the model is expecting for training.

5.5.3 Caching

Another cool trick that we can utilize to increase our pipeline's performance is caching. **Caching is a way to temporarily store data in memory or in local storage**, in order to avoid repeating operations like reading and extraction. Since each data instance will be fed into the model more than once (one time for each epoch), why not store it into the memory? That is exactly what we can do using the `cache` function from `tf.data`.

```
train = train.cache()
```

Each transformation is applied before the `cache` function is executed, and only on the first epoch. The caveat here is that we have to be very careful on the limitations of our resources, to avoid overloading the cache with too much data. However, if we have complex transformations, it is usually preferred to do them offline rather than executing them on a training job and cache the data. Also note this is not a good idea if our transformations are stochastic.

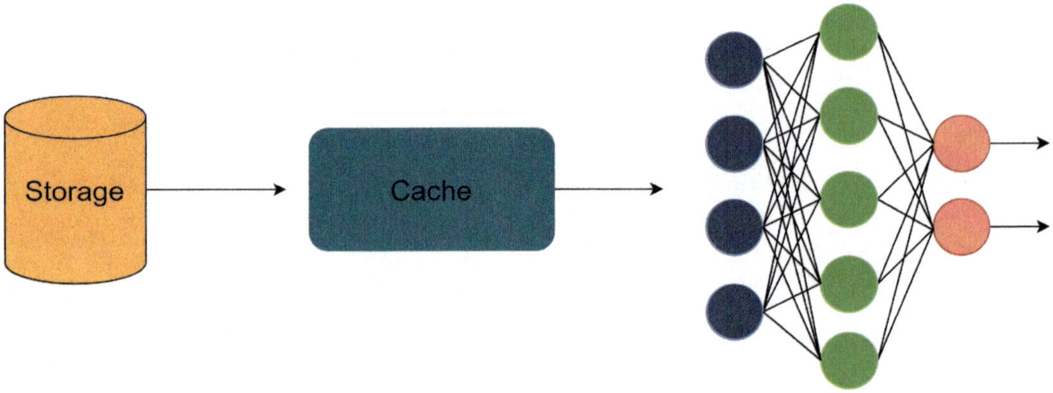

Figure 5.4: Caching

Generally, this is all we need to know about building data pipelines and making them as efficient as possible. Our whole pipeline is finally in place and it looks like this:

```
data = tfds.load(
    data_config.path, with_info=data_config.load_with_info
)

train = dataset['train'].map(
     lambda image: DataLoader.preprocess_train(image,image_size),
     num_parallel_calls=tf.data.experimental.AUTOTUNE
 )

train_dataset = train
    .shuffle(buffer_size)\
    .batch(batch_size)\
```

```
    .cache()\
    .repeat()

model.fit(train_dataset)
```

However, before we proceed with the training, I want to discuss another very important topic that you may or may not need in your everyday coding life. Streaming. In fact, with streaming we go back to the extraction phase of our pipeline, but I feel like I need to include it here for completion.

5.5.4 Streaming

First of all, what are we trying to achieve with streaming? And second, what is streaming?

Motivation: There are use cases where we don't know the full size of our data as they might come from an unbounded source.

For example, we can acquire them by an external API, or extract them from a database of another service that we don't know many details about. Imagine for example that we have an Internet of Things (IoT) application where we collect data from different sensors, and we apply some sort of ML model to them. In this scenario, we don't really know the full size of the data and we can assume that we have an infinite source that will generate data forever. So how do we handle that and how we can incorporate the data into a data pipeline?

Here is when streaming comes really handy. But what is streaming?

Streaming is a method of transmitting and receiving data (over a computer network) as a steady, continuous flow, allowing playback to start while the rest of the data is still being received.

What is happening behind the scenes, is that the sender and the receiver open a connection which remains active for as long as they need. Then the sender sends very small chunks of our data through the connection and the receiver gets them and reassembles them into their original form.

Can you now see how useful that can be for us? **We can open a connection with an external data source and keep processing the data and training our model on them for as long as they come**.

To make our lives easier, we can use an open-source library called Tensorflow I/O. Tensorflow I/O supports many different data sources not included in the original Tensorflow code such as BigQuery, Kafka and multiple formats like audio, medical images, and genomic data. And of course, the output is fully compatible with `tf.data`. As a result, we can apply all the functions and tricks we talked about.

Let's see an example of when our data come from Kafka. For those of you who don't know, Kafka is a high-performance distributed messaging system that is being used widely in the industry.

```
import tensorflow_io.kafka as kafka_io
dataset = kafka_io.KafkaDataset (
    'topic', server = "our server", group=" our group"
)
dataset = dataset.map(...)
```

Don't hang up too much on the Kafka details. Tools come and go. The essence is that it makes streaming incredibly simple.

Chapter 6

Training

In this chapter:

1. How to train your model locally
2. How to train in the cloud
3. How to train on multiple machines

Training is undoubtedly the most important part of developing an ML application. Usually, the first step is to define an achievable and appropriate performance level. In this process, you will deal with how the hyperparameters should be adjusted and other architectural changes. In general, most ML research engineers spend quite some time on training, experimenting with different models, tuning their architecture, and discovering the best metrics and losses for their problem.

In this chapter, we will build a custom trainer for our UNet model. This time we will go through the whole development lifecycle step by step. You will learn how to program the entire `Trainer` class as you would do in your day to day job. It is also a great opportunity to apply all the discussed best practices. Finally, you will explore how you can build highly performant and highly maintainable software in real time.

So be prepared for a lot of code this time. Without further ado, let's get started.

6.1 Building a trainer

First things first. Let's write our initial training code for our semantic segmentation example. All we have, in the following snippet, is boilerplate Keras code, which includes the model's compilation and fitting.

```
self.model.compile(
     optimizer=self.config.train.optimizer.type,
     loss=tf.keras.losses
        .SparseCategoricalCrossentropy(from_logits=True),
     metrics=self.config.train.metrics)

LOG.info('Training started')
model_history = self.model.fit(
    self.train_dataset,
    epochs = self.epoches,
    steps_per_epoch = self.steps_per_epoch,
    validation_steps = self.validation_steps,
    validation_data=self.test_dataset
)

return model_history.history['loss'],
    model_history.history['val_loss']
```

We chose `SparseCategoricalCrossentropy` as our loss, `Adam` as our optimizer and `SparseCategoricalAccuracy` for our main metric.

To keep things simpler and cleaner, I think that we can include the above code in a new `Trainer` class. That's why in the above code snippet some variables are prefixed with `self`. The `Trainer` class will be invoked inside the `train()` method of our `UNet` class as defined in the section 4.1.2.

```
class UNet(BaseModel):
    """Unet Model Class"""

    def __init__(self, config):
        . . .
        self.epoches = self.config.train.epoches



    . . .
```

```python
    def train(self):
        """Compiles and trains the model"""

        LOG.info('Training started')
        optimizer = tf.keras.optimizers.Adam()
        loss =
            tf.keras.losses.SparseCategoricalCrossentropy(
                from_logits=True
            )
        metrics = tf.keras.metrics.SparseCategoricalAccuracy()

        trainer = Trainer(self.model, self.train_dataset, loss,
            optimizer, metrics, self.epoches
        )
        trainer.train()
```

All I'm doing here is defining the optimizer, the loss, the metrics, and pass them along with the model and the dataset, in a trainer class called `Trainer`. The `Trainer` will be the main class that handles the model's training. Once we create a new instance of the class, we can call an internal `trainer.train()` method triggering the beginning of our training.

A good practice is to try and keep the `Trainer` class unaware of all the other components of the application such as the model and the data. Each class should have a sole purpose and perform only a single thing. No further dependencies on other elements. This is the "separation of concerns" principle, a vital concept that ensures the maintainability and scalability of our software.

6.1.1 Creating a custom training loop

So, let's dive into the `Trainer` class and try to improve it. Each trainer instance depends on only six things: model, input data, loss function, optimizer, metric and the number of epochs.

```python
class Trainer:
    def __init__(self, model, input, loss_fn, optimizer,
                 metric, epochs):
        self.model = model
        self.input = input
        self.loss_fn = loss_fn
        self.optimizer = optimizer
        self.metric = metric
```

```
        self.epochs = epochs
```

Nothing fancy here, as you can see. Inside the `Trainer` class, we also need a `train` method, which will have the overall training functionality, and a `train_step` method that will contain only a single training step.

In production, it's often preferred to have a custom training loop instead of relying on high-level APIs such as Keras, because we are able to tune every little detail and have full control over the process.

In the `train_step` method, we perform the actual training of a single batch. First, we need to get the training variables, aka the model weights, and extract the input/label from the batch.

```
trainable_variables = self.model.trainable_variables
inputs, labels = batch
```

Then, we need to feed the input into the model and calculate the loss based on the labels and the prediction of the UNet.

```
with tf.GradientTape() as tape:
     predictions = self.model(inputs)
     step_loss = self.loss_fn(labels, predictions
```

We are using `tf.GradientTape()` from Tensorflow to capture the gradients during the step. Then, we can apply them into the optimizer and change the weights accordingly.

```
grads = tape.gradient(step_loss, trainable_variables)

self.optimizer.apply_gradients(zip(grads, trainable_variables))
```

In essence, we are running the back-propagation algorithm by taking advantage of the APIs provided by Tensorflow.

Finally, we need to update our metric and return the step loss and the predictions to be consumed by the `train` function.

```
self.metric.update_state(labels, predictions)
return step_loss, predictions
```

And at last we have something like this:

```
def train_step(self, batch):
```

```
    trainable_variables = self.model.trainable_variables
    inputs, labels = batch

    with tf.GradientTape() as tape:
        predictions = self.model(inputs)
        step_loss = self.loss_fn(labels, predictions)

    grads = tape.gradient(step_loss, trainable_variables)
    self.optimizer.apply_gradients(zip(grads, trainable_variables))
    self.metric.update_state(labels, predictions)

    return step_loss, predictions
```

Now, let's go to the **train** method. The **train** method will simply be a "for-loop" that iterates over the number of epochs and a secondary "for-loop" inside, that trains every batch (this is our training step).

```
def train(self):
    for epoch in range(self.epochs):
        LOG.info(f'Start epoch {epoch}')

        for step, training_batch in enumerate(self.input):
            step_loss, predictions = self.train_step(training_batch)
            LOG.info("Loss at step %d: %.2f" % (step, step_loss))

            train_acc = self.metric.result()
            LOG.info(f'Saved checkpoint: {save_path}')
```

As I mentioned before, all there is here are two "for-loops" and a lot of logging. Providing logs is vital so we can have a clear image of what's going on during training. In this way, we are able to stop or continue the training based on the info we received from them, and to recognize errors and bugs immediately. The `LOG` variable is a constant defined on the top of the file which initializes a logging utility as presented in Chapter 4.

```
LOG = get_logger('trainer')
```

A couple of observations before we proceed: First of all, the input is a Tensorflow dataset (`tf.data`) and, as you can see, we can iterate over it as we will do for a normal collection (remember iterators?). Secondly, I'm sure you noticed that we capture both the loss and the accuracy throughout the entire program. This is not just to provide logs but also to enable visualization of our training using Tensorboard. Thirdly, we need a way to save the state of our training periodically because deep learning models can be trained for a lot of time. This can be hours, days or even weeks. To avoid losing our weights and to be able to reuse a trained model afterwards, we need to incorporate some sort of checkpointing functionality. Luckily, there is an already built-in function for that.

6.1.2 Training checkpoints

Saving the current state in checkpoints is actually quite easy. All we have to do is define a checkpoint manager and an initial checkpoint to continue the training from there. If it is the first time we train the model, this will be empty, otherwise it will be loaded from an external folder. So, in our `__init__` function, we have:

```
self.checkpoint = tf.train.Checkpoint(
    optimizer=optimizer, model=model
)

self.checkpoint_manager = tf.train.CheckpointManager(
     self.checkpoint, './tf_ckpts'
)
```

The checkpoint is defined by the optimizer and the model. The checkpoint manager is constructed using the initial checkpoint and a folder path to save the checkpoints. To store the current state in an external file, this is all we need to do:

```
save_path = self.checkpoint_manager.save()

LOG.info(f'Saved checkpoint: {save_path}')
```

We place this usually at the end of each epoch or after a subset of epochs is completed.

6.1.3 Saving the trained model

Once the training is finished, we want to store the final state of the trainable parameters along with various metadata. Again, this is quite straightforward in Tensorflow and can be done in a couple of lines:

```
self.model_save_path = 'saved_models/'

save_path = os.path.join(self.model_save_path, "unet/1/")
```

```
tf.saved_model.save(self.model, save_path)
```

And of course, loading a saved model couldn't be that hard either.

```
model = tf.saved_model.load(save_path)
```

6.1.4 Visualizing the training with Tensorboard

If you are a visual person like me, logs are not the easiest thing to look at when trying to get a sense of how your training is proceeding. It would be much nicer to have a way to visualize the process and look at charts instead of lines of logs. If you aren't aware, Tensorboard is a way to plot the metrics captured during training and create beautiful graphs. It's also a very good way to explore the computational graph and get a high-level image of our entire architecture.

Another useful tool is `tf.summary`. It is an elegant built-in method to write our metrics into logs that can be later utilized by Tensorboard. We can build a summary writer using an external path like this:

```
self.train_log_dir = 'logs/gradient_tape/'

self.train_summary_writer = tf.summary.create_file_writer(
    self.train_log_dir
)
```

And at the end of each epoch, we can use the writer to save the current metrics:

```
def _write_summary(self, loss, epoch):
    with self.train_summary_writer.as_default():
        tf.summary.scalar('loss', loss, step=epoch)
        tf.summary.scalar(
            'accuracy', self.metric.result(), step=epoch
        )
```

Some things to notice here:

- `tf.summary.scalar` creates a file and writes the metrics under the hood.
- The logs are saved in a binary format so we can't open the file and read them.
- We can either pass the metric as an argument on the function (as we do for the loss) or we can utilize `tf.metric`. The latter stores the state inside the computational graph.

Then, we can update the metric inside the graph using:

```
self.metric.update_state(labels, predictions)
```

And then get the current state by:

```
self.metric.result()
```

Where:

```
self.metric = tf.keras.metrics.SparseCategoricalAccuracy()
```

Once we have the summary written, we can spin up a Tensorboard instance in our localhost by executing the following command:

```
$ tensorboard --logdir logs/gradient_tape
```

The Tensorboard should appear right afterwards as it is shown in Figure 6.1.

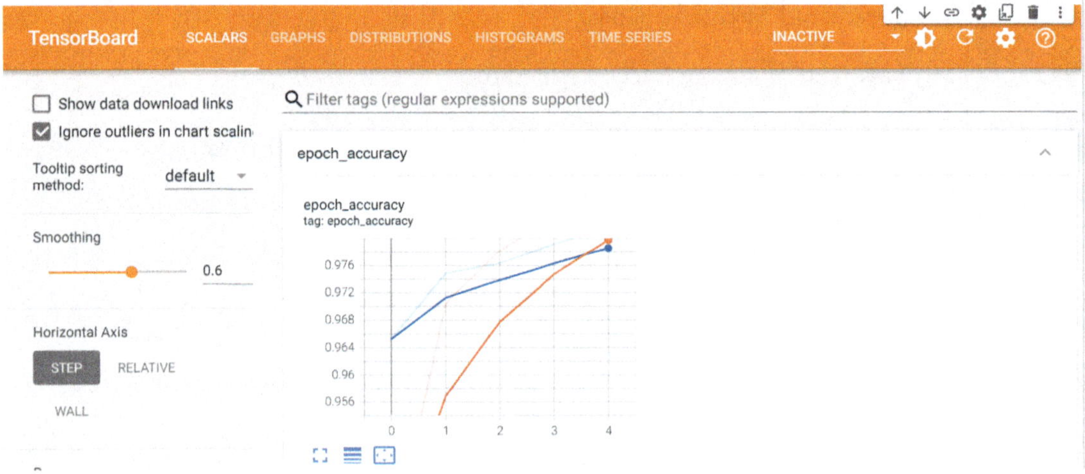

Figure 6.1: Tensorboard example

Tensorboard will continue to print the metrics as the training is running. I highly recommend spending some time with it. There are a lot of handy stuff you can do. It will provide you with some intuitions on how the training is proceeding.

6.1.5 Model validation

Before we wrap up this section, I would like to mention one thing that we haven't touched upon: validation. Most of the time, after training, we apply a validation procedure so we can be sure that our results are correct and the model is not overfitting the training data. All the principles that we have already outlined also apply here. To do so, we would again need to have a `test` and a `test_step` similar to `train` and `train_step`. Afterwards we can use `tf.metrics`, logs and Tensorboard. The only difference is that we wouldn't need to compute the gradients.

Ideally, the validation and test set should be sampled independently from the same statistical data distribution.

Note that test and validation are not the same thing, they do, however, share the same class methods `test` and `test_step`. The validation data provide us with a hint on how the model will perform during testing. We often compare the validation performance of different ML architectures, or the exact same model with different hyperparameters. You can think of it like a student's homework before the final test exam of the year.

Undeniably, the best practice is to split your training data into 3 sets. You are probably wondering how to do that in a statistically proper way. In general, rely on random splitting only as a last resort. Otherwise, try to build intuitions based on the available data. The key principle is to obtain the test and validation samples from a distribution that will resemble the expected user data after deployment.

In the image segmentation use case, if the end users were to send us animal pictures via their smartphones, it would be awesome to use images from smartphones as our validation and test set. There are cases that you would need to label your own data if possible, or even ask domain experts to label some data for you. As for the training data, using a slightly different data distribution can be justified because of the data availability. In any case, you have to be aware of the distribution shift phenomenon between training and testing data. The distribution of smartphone images will be much more diverse compared to a static dataset with animals mostly placed on the centre of the image that is collected from the web.

To sum up, the closer the test and validation data are to the data that will be provided by the end users, the better. The validation will help us choose the best model and hyperparameters and a representative test set will give us a fair estimation of the production performance.

6.2 Training in the cloud

When it comes to training, there are many obstacles that we need to overcome. We have to acquire lots of data, to fine tune our architecture and hyperparameters, to improve the accuracy, to build logging and visualization systems. However, one of the most frequent struggles is the lack of hardware resources. Most of us don't own a super high-end GPU or don't have access to a cluster of PCs, so we are forced to wait hours on each training iteration before we evaluate our model.

I also understand that some of us are tempted to buy a high-end GPU. And to be honest with you I have already tried it. Nevertheless, there is a much easier way to train our models and I'm sure you're aware of that. It's called cloud computing. Cloud providers such as Google Cloud, Amazon Web Services (AWS) and Microsoft Azure are excellent examples of low cost, high-end infrastructure.

In this section, we will take our UNet and deploy it in the Google Cloud. We will actually run a full training job. The goal is to take the custom trainer we developed in the previous section, transfer it to a cloud Virtual Machine (VM) instance, and execute it in the remote environment.

"What is an instance?", you may think. We will get there, don't worry.

Regarding the structure of the section, I think I should take it step by step and explain the following important topics:

- Starting with cloud computing
- Creating a VM instance
- Connecting to the VM instance
- Transferring files to the VM instance
- Running the training remotely
- Accessing training data from a remote environment

6.2.1 Getting started with cloud computing

Cloud computing is the **on-demand** delivery of IT resources via the internet. Instead of buying and maintaining physical servers and data centres, we can access infrastructure such as computer power and storage from cloud providers.

About 90% of all companies in the world use some form of cloud service today. I hope that's enough to convince you about the power of the cloud. The most astonishing thing about it, is that we literally have access to a huge variety of different systems and applications that would be unimaginable to maintain on our own.

For our use case, we're going to need only one of all these services, **Compute Engine**. Compute Engine lets us use Virtual Machine instances hosted in the Google servers which are maintained by Google engineers.

A Virtual Machine (VM) is an emulation of a computer system. Virtual machines are based on computer architectures and provide the functionality of a physical computer.

Their implementations may involve specialized hardware, software, or a combination of them.

In essence, we borrow a small PC in a Google data center, install whatever operating system and software we may want (aka build a VM), and execute our software remotely.

Ok now that we know the basics, let's proceed with a hands-on approach. If you haven't created a Google cloud account by now, feel free to do that. All you have to do is go to Google Cloud's website and register an account. A credit card is required for security reasons, but it won't be charged for at least a year or if you surpass the free quotas. As a new user you can enjoy a full 300$ free credit (at the time of writing this book).

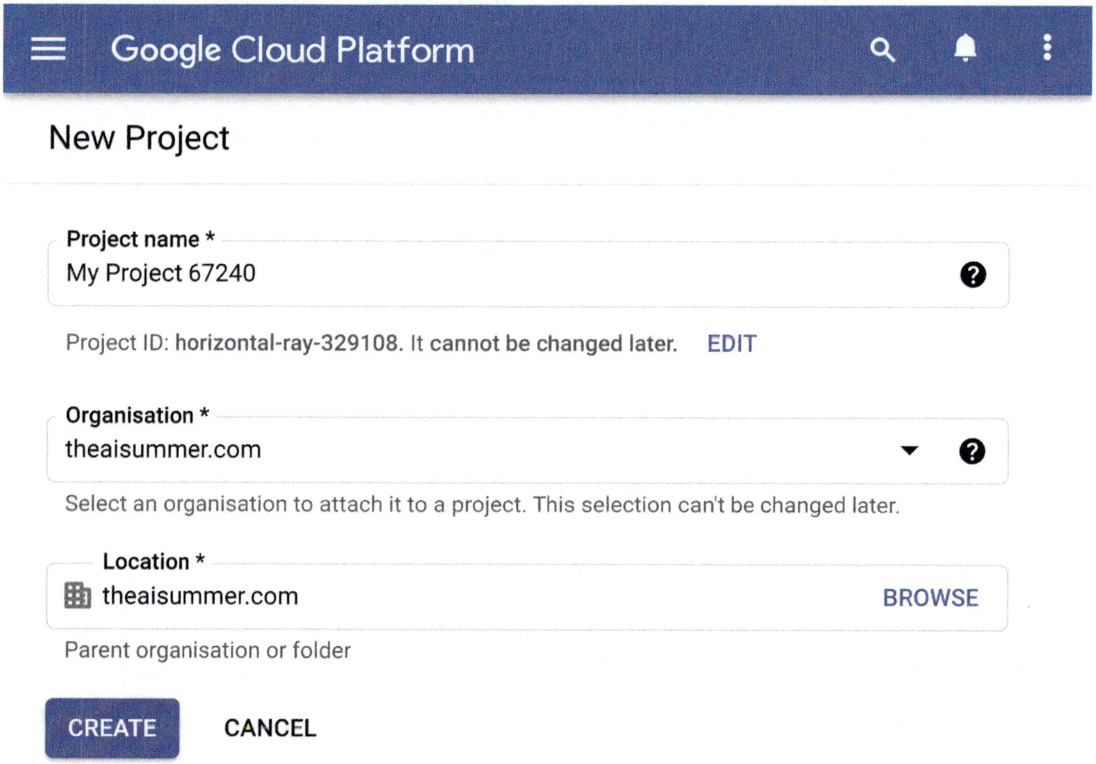

Figure 6.2: Create a project on Google cloud

Note: In most cases the cloud providers follow a pay-as-you-go pricing model, meaning that we get charged depending on how many resources we use.

6.2.2 Creating a VM instance

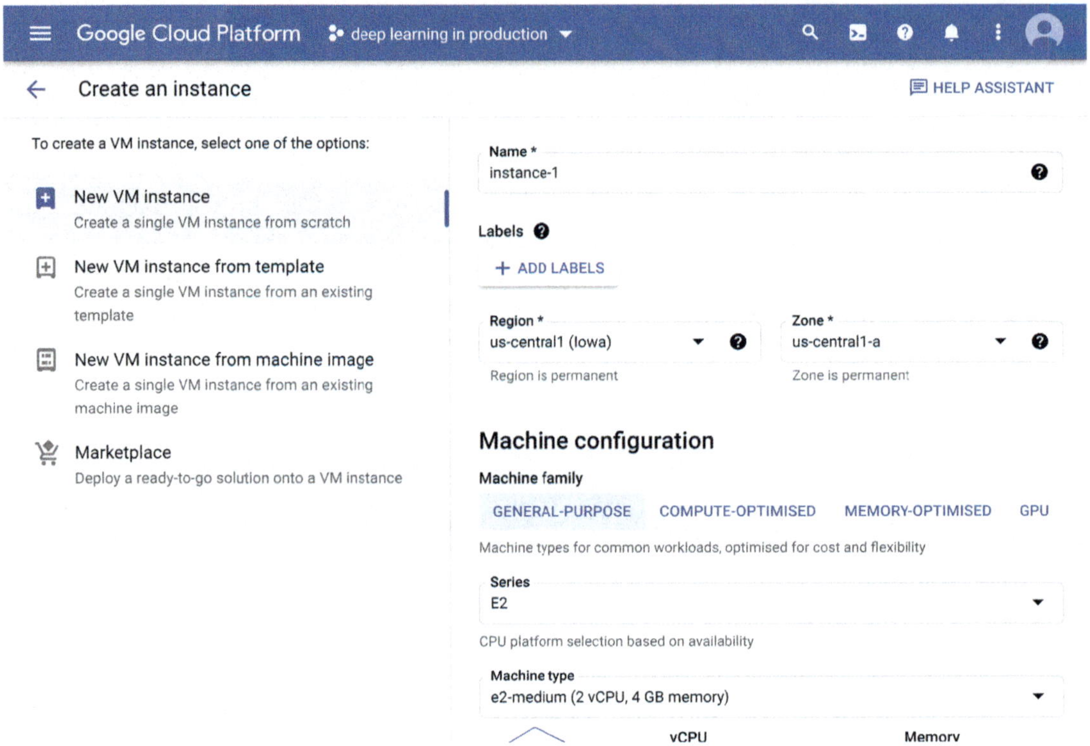

Figure 6.3: Create a VM instance on Google cloud

Once you have a Google Cloud account, it's time to create a new project to host our application by clicking on the top left button, "New project", and naming it whatever you like. You should see something like the Figure 6.2.

When the project is initialized, we can navigate to Compute Engine > VM instances from the sidebar on the left and create a new VM as shown in the Figure 6.3.

We can customize the instance in any fashion we like. We can choose our CPU, our RAM, and optionally add a GPU. I'll keep things simple and select a standard CPU with 4 GB of memory and an Nvidia Tesla K80. Of course, we can pick our own OS. I will use Ubuntu's 20.04 minimal image with a 10GB disk size.

We can also enable some extra things like deploying a container to the instance or allow traffic from the Internet, but let's not deal with them right now. Just for completion, let's mention that we can allow HTTP or HTTPS traffic to our instance. More on that later.

In the next chapters we will see more of the additional functionalities like deploying a container to the instance, allowing traffic from the Internet.

6.2.3 Connecting to the VM instance

Ok great, we have our instance up and running. It's time to start using it. We can connect to it using standard SSH by clicking the SSH button. This will open a new browser window and give us access to the Google machine.

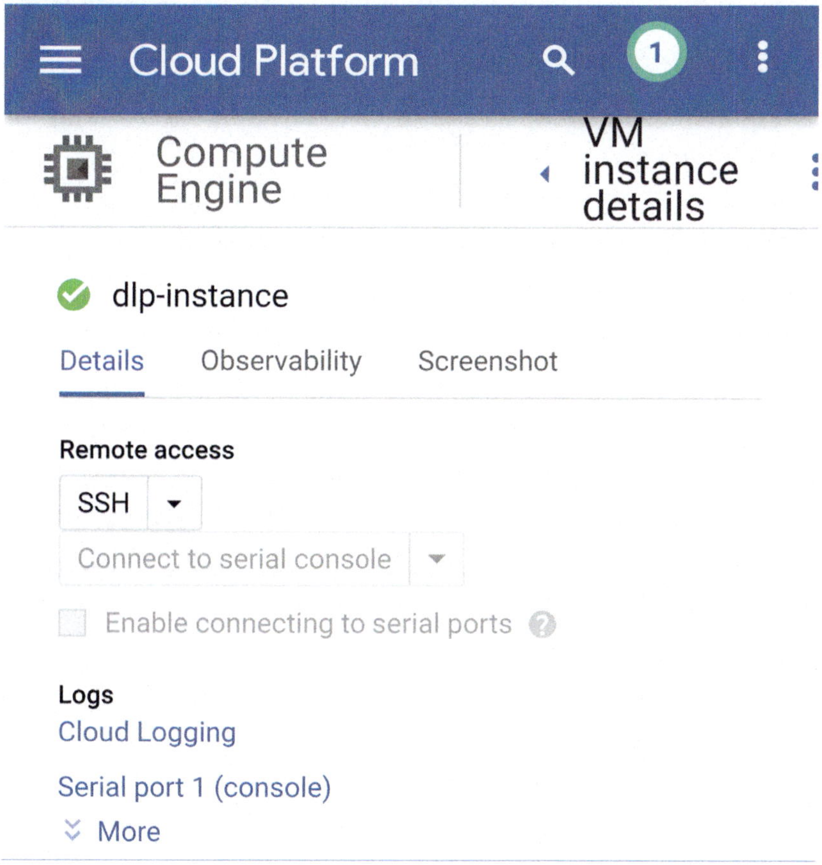

Figure 6.4: Connection to a remote VM instance

We can literally connect through a terminal to a remote machine in Google servers. We can now install whatever we want as we would normally do in our laptop.

6.2.4 Transferring files to the VM instance

The next step is to **transfer our data and code into the remote machine**. Google Cloud uses a specialized command called `gcloud` that handles many things

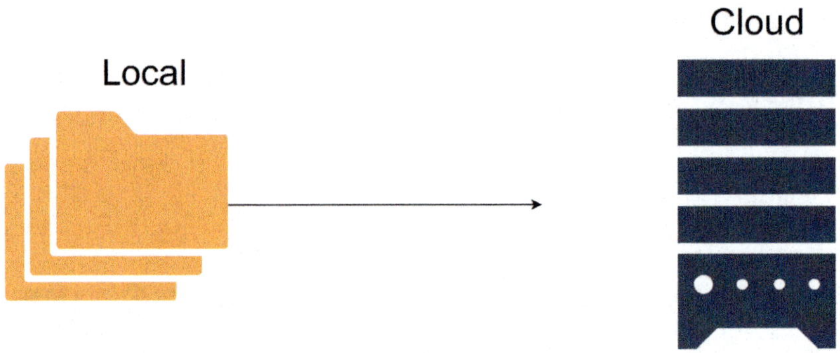

Figure 6.5: Files transfer from local workstation to cloud

such as authentication (using SHH under the hood). A similar command exists in almost all cloud providers, so the following steps have a similar logic.

SSH is a protocol that uses encryption to secure the connection between a client and a server and allow us to safely connect to a remote machine.

We can very easily download and install the Google Cloud SDK in our local terminal.

```
$ curl -O https://dl.google.com/dl/cloudsdk/channels/rapid
/downloads/google-cloud-sdk-344.0.0-linux-x86_64.tar.gz

$ tar xvzf ./google-cloud-sdk/

$ ./google-cloud-sdk/install.sh

$ ./google-cloud-sdk/bin/gcloud init
```

After that, we can connect to the instance from our local terminal using:

```
$ gcloud compute ssh training-instance
```

Note that we can close the connection and return to the local terminal by typing `exit`.

To transfer the files from our local system to the remote instance, we can use the `gcloud scp` command. I will transfer the whole project in the instance so we can run the training the same way we did locally.

```
$ gcloud compute scp --recurse
   /home/aisummer/src/Deep-Learning-in-Production/
```

```
  training-instance:app
```

6.2.5 Running the training remotely

Now all we have to do is execute the `main.py` and the training will start immediately. But first, we need to install the Python libraries. If you have included all the required dependencies in the `requirements.txt`, just run `apt-get` python and `pip install` all the libraries that are listed in the requirements.txt file:

```
sudo apt install python3-pip
pip install -r requirements.txt
```

Tip: Google Cloud provides a variety of ready-to-use instances for various use cases. When we create the instance, we can choose a premade template that contains all of our essential libraries and languages.

Once the training is complete, we can transfer back the saved model's weights and perhaps the logs. Note that as we did locally in the previous section, we can again monitor the logs during training. We can even set up Tensorboard remotely. We can literally do anything we would do on our own laptop. But with a lot more resources and ready-made solutions.

```
$ gcloud compute scp --recurse  training-instance:app
  /home/aisummer/src/ Deep-Learning-in-Production/
```

6.2.6 Accessing training data from a remote environment

Those who have an inherent talent to observe the details, might have noticed that I deliberately haven't mentioned data up to this point. Until now, I assumed that we bake the data within our application and upload them in the VM instance alongside with the code. So, when the training kicks off, it reads the pet images from a local path. Of course, that's not very efficient and should be avoided.

A better option might be to **store the data in the cloud** as well, but outside of our computing environment. All cloud providers have an object storage solution that enables us to do exactly that. AWS calls it S3, Azure calls it Azure Storage, and Google calls it Cloud Storage (GCS).

Object storages are computer data storage architectures that manage data as distinct units called objects, as opposed to other architectures which manage data as hierarchical files or blocks. Each object has the data, some metadata and a globally unique identifier. Cloud storage provides security, scalability, flexible management and resilience.

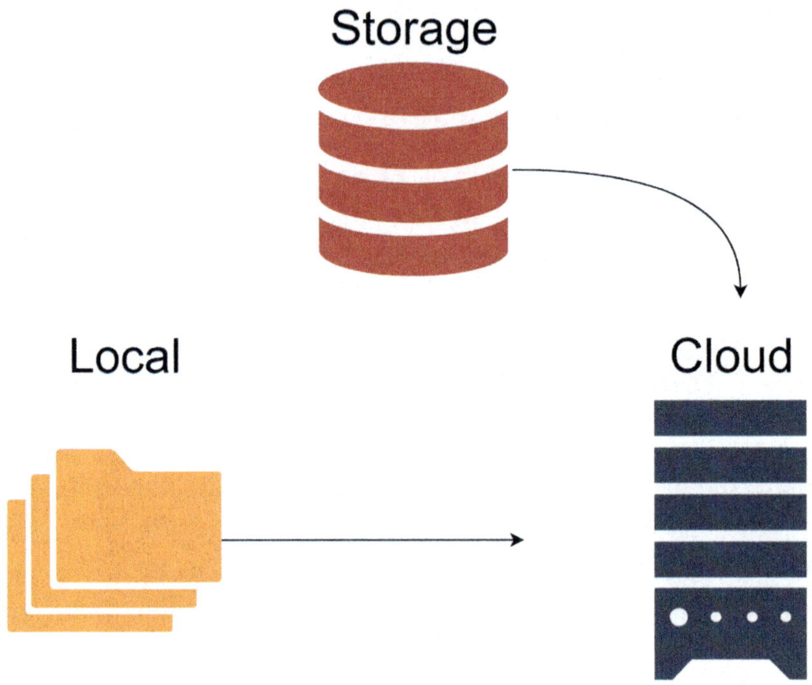

Figure 6.6: Object storage for storing data on cloud

Objects are organized in **buckets** and a project can contain multiple buckets. Buckets can be created and organized at your own discretion. For example, in our case, we can create a bucket called "deep-learning-in-production-data" and save all of our pet images there. In fact, that's exactly what we're going to do.

We can create a bucket very easily by navigating to the storage service and click "create bucket" to open the bucket creation form shown below.

Obviously, we can have many buckets to organize our data as we want. Each has a distinct name, a location, a storage class and all of our objects.

When the bucket is created, we can upload an object directly from the User Interface (UI). We can absolutely do all of that using the terminal or even HTTP requests, but I personally see no value in doing that here.

To summarize, we have our data uploaded and it's time to use them in our training. This can be done very easily using `tf.data` and input pipelines as we explained in Chapter 5.

```
filenames = 'gs://deep-learning-in-production-training-data
/oxford_iiit_pet/*'
```

```
filepath = tf.io.gfile.glob(filenames)
dataset = tf.data.TFRecordDataset(filepath)
```

Or we can use `tdfs` and do something like this:

```
tfds.load(
     name="oxford_iiit_pet",
     data_dir="gs://deep-learning-in-production-training-data/"
)
```

And that's it. We incorporate this small change into our input pipeline code, redeploy our application into the instance, and it will automatically load the data from cloud storage into our model during training. The best part is that cloud storage is ridiculously cheap.

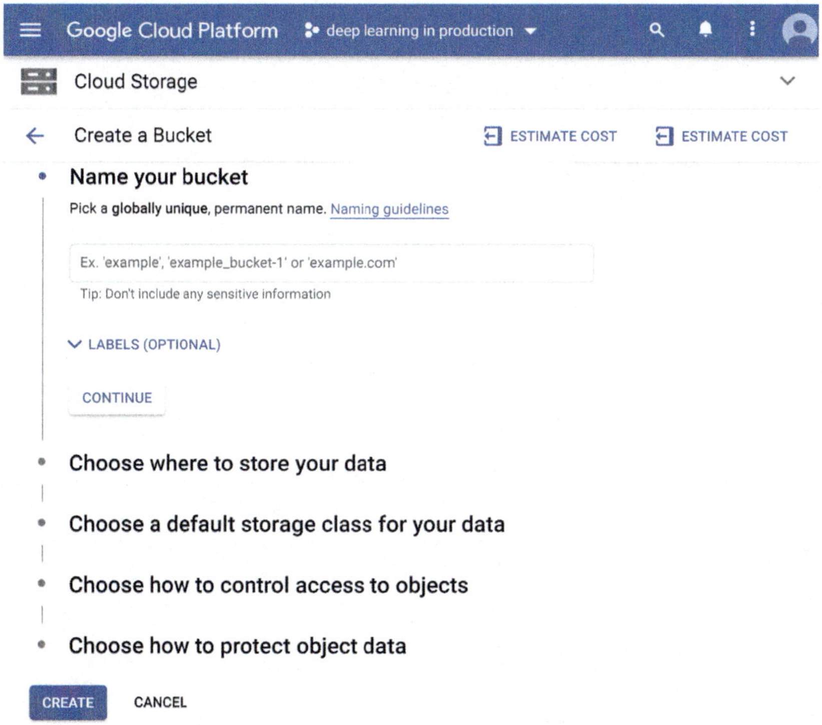

Figure 6.7: Creation of bucket in Google cloud storage

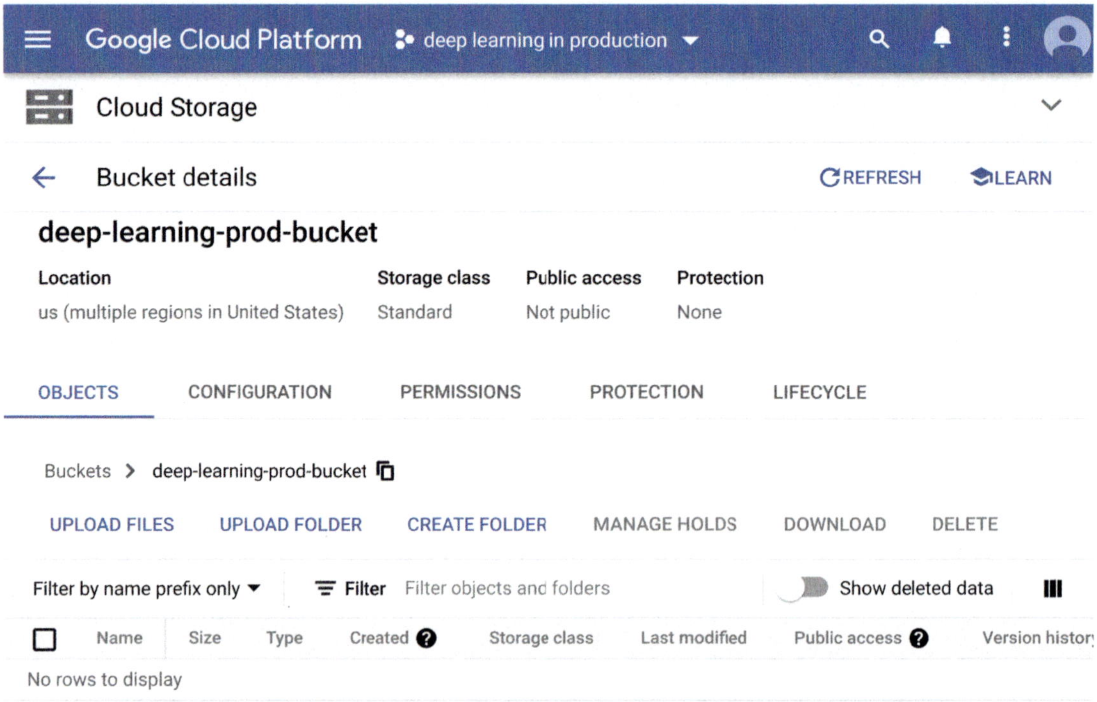

Figure 6.8: Google storage bucket details

6.3 Distributed training

In a significant number of use cases, deep learning training can be performed in a single machine, on a single GPU, with relatively high performance and speed. However, there are times that we need more speed. Such examples include scenarios when our data may be way too large to fit on a single machine, or our hardware is not capable enough to handle the training. As a result, we are forced to **scale out**.

Scaling out means adding more GPUs to our machine or perhaps using multiple machines inside a cluster. Therefore, we need some way to **distribute our training efficiently**. There are multiple strategies that we can use to distribute our training and the choice depends heavily on our specific use case, data and model.

In this section I will attempt to outline all the different strategies in detail. The goal is to provide an overall view of the area. The main objective is to provide you with the guidelines so that you can choose the best one for your application. Finally, I will also present some code of those distribution strategies using Tensorflow. Nonetheless, most of the concepts apply to the other deep learning frameworks as well.

6.3.1 Data vs model parallelism

The two major schools on distributed training are data parallelism and model parallelism.

In the first scenario, we scatter our data throughout a set of GPUs or machines, and we perform the training loop in all of them either synchronously or asynchronously (you will understand what this means later). I would dare to say that 95% of all training is done using this concept.

Of course, it depends heavily on the network speed as there is a lot of communication between clusters and GPUs, but most of the time this is the ideal solution. Its advantages include:

- universality because we can use it for every model and every cluster.
- fast compilation as the software is written to perform specifically on that single cluster.
- full utilization of hardware.

However, there are cases that the model is too big to fit in a single machine. Then model parallelism might be a better idea. Model parallelism enables us to split our model into different segments and train each segment into a different machine. The most frequent use case is modern Natural Language Processing (NLP) models that contain billion parameters.

6.3.2 Training in a single machine

Before we continue, let's pause for a minute and remind ourselves what training in a single machine with a single CPU looks like. Let's imagine that we have a simple neural network with two layers and three nodes in each layer.

1. Each trainable component has its own weights and biases.
2. A training step begins with processing our data.
3. We feed the processed data into our network.
4. The network predicts the output (forward pass).
5. We then compare the prediction with the desired label by computing the loss.
6. In the backward pass we compute the gradients and update the weights based on the gradients.
7. Repeat step 2 with the new batch of data until training is terminated.

In the easiest scenario, a single CPU with multiple cores is enough to support the training. Keep in mind that we can also take advantage of multithreading. To speed things up, we add a GPU accelerator and transfer our data to the GPU's memory. The next step is to add multiple GPUs, and finally to expand to multiple machines with multiple GPUs on each one, all connected over a network.

To make sure that we are all in the same page here are some basic notations:

- **Worker**: a separate machine that contains a CPU and one or more GPUs.
- **Accelerator**: a single GPU or TPU.
- **All-reduce**: a distributed algorithm that aggregates all the trainable parameters from different workers or accelerators. Essentially, it receives the weights from all workers and aggregates them to compute the final weights.

Since most strategies apply on both worker level and accelerator level, you may see me use the term "device". This indicates that the distribution may happen between different machines or different GPUs.

Cool. Now that we know our basics it's time to proceed with the different strategies for data parallelism .

We can roughly distinguish the strategies into two big categories: synchronous (sync) and asynchronous (async).

In sync training, all devices train over different slices of input data and aggregate the gradients in each step. In async training, all devices are independently trained over the input data and update variables in an asynchronous manner.

Let's clarify those terms.

6.3.3 Synchronous training

In synchronous training, we send different slices of data into each device. **Each device has a full replica of the model** and it is trained only on a part of the data. The forward pass begins at the same time in all devices. They all compute different gradients. At this moment all the devices are communicating with each other and they are aggregating the gradients using the **all-reduce algorithm**. The final gradients are sent back to all the devices. Each device then continues with the backward pass, updating the local copy of the weights normally.

The next forward pass doesn't begin until all the variables have been updated. And that's why it is synchronous. At each point in time, all the devices have the exact same weights despite the fact that they produced different gradients as they trained on different data; because they are updated based on the gradients on all the data.

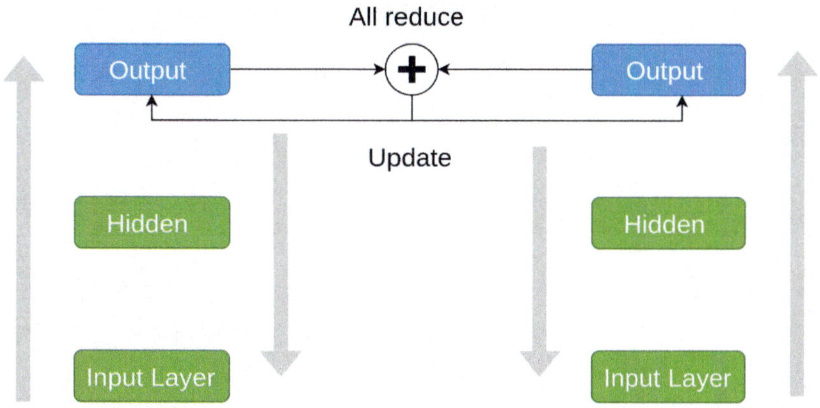

Figure 6.9: Distributed update of weights with an all-reduce algorithm

Tensorflow refers to this strategy as **mirrored strategy** and it supports two different types:

- The `tf.distribute.MirroredStrategy` is designed to run on many accelerators in the same worker.
- The `tf.distribute.experimental.MultiWorkerMirroredStrategy` is for use on multiple workers.

The basic principles behind the two of them are exactly the same.

Let us see some code. Remember that our custom training loop consists of two functions, the `train` function and the `train_step` function. The first one iterates over the number of epochs and runs the `train_step` on each one, while the second performs a single pass on one batch of data.

```
def train_step(self, batch):
    trainable_variables = self.model.trainable_variables
    inputs, labels = batch
    with tf.GradientTape() as tape:
        predictions = self.model(inputs)
        step_loss = self.loss_fn(labels, predictions)

        grads = tape.gradient(step_loss, trainable_variables)
        self.optimizer.apply_gradients(
            zip(grads, trainable_variables)
        )
```

```python
        return step_loss, predictions

def train(self):
    for epoch in range(self.epoches):
        for step, training_batch in enumerate(self.input):
            step_loss, predictions = self.train_step(training_batch
```

However, distributing our training using a custom training loop is not that straightforward because it requires to use some special functions to aggregate losses and gradients. That's why I will use the classic high-level Keras API. Besides, our goal in this section is to outline the concepts rather than to focus on the actual code and the Tensorflow intricacies.

So, when you think of the training code, you will imagine something like this:

```python
def train(self):
    """Compiles and trains the model"""
    self.model.compile(
        optimizer=self.config.train.optimizer.type,
        loss=tf.keras.losses.SparseCategoricalCrossentropy(
            from_logits=True
        ),
        metrics=self.config.train.metrics
    )

    model_history = self.model.fit(
                        self.train_dataset,
                        epochs = self.epochs,
                        steps_per_epoch = self.steps_per_epoch,
                        validation_steps = self.validation_steps,
                        validation_data = self.test_dataset
    )

    return model_history.history['loss'],
        model_history.history['val_loss']
```

And for building our UNet model, we have:

```python
self.model = tf.keras.Model(inputs=inputs, outputs=x)
```

Mirrored Strategy

According to Tensorflow docs:

"Each variable in the model is mirrored across all the replicas. Together, these variables form a single conceptual variable called `MirroredVariable`. These variables are kept in sync with each other by applying identical updates."

I guess that explains the name.

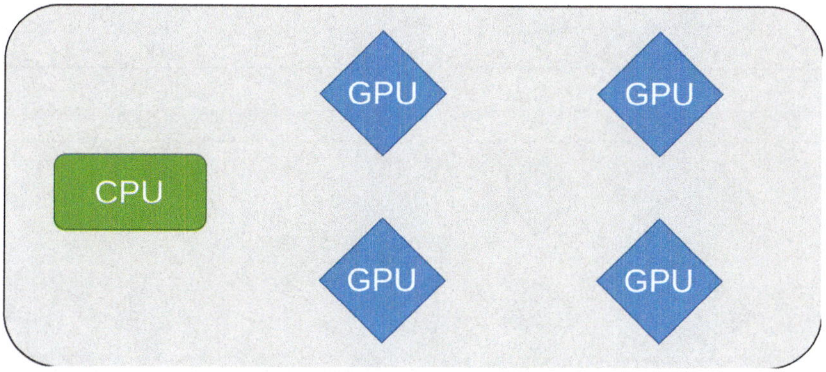

Figure 6.10: Mirrored strategy

We can initialize it by writing:

```
mirrored_strategy = tf.distribute.MirroredStrategy(
    devices=["/gpu:0", "/gpu:1"]
)
```

As you may have understood, we will run the training on two GPUs, which are passed as arguments inside the class instance. Then all we have to do is wrap our code with the strategy scope like below:

```
with mirrored_strategy.scope():
    self.model = tf.keras.Model(inputs=inputs, outputs=x)
    self.model.compile(...)
    self.model.fit(...)
```

The `scope()` makes sure that all variables are mirrored in all of our devices and that the block underneath is distribution-aware.

Multi Worker Mirrored Strategy

Similar to `MirroredStrategy`, `MultiWorkerMirroredStrategy` implements the training on many workers. Again, it creates copies of all variables across the workers and runs the training in a sync manner.

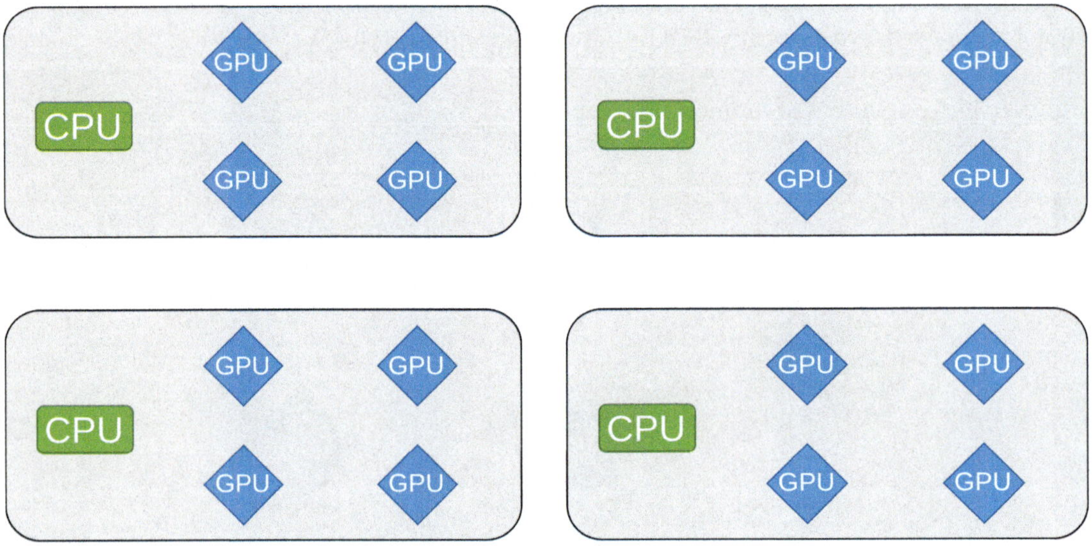

Figure 6.11: Multi worker mirrored strategy

This time we use json configs to define our workers:

```
os.environ["TF_CONFIG"] = json.dumps(
    {
        "cluster":{
            "worker": ["host1:port", "host2:port", "host3:port"]
        },
        "task":{
            "type": "worker",
            "index": 1
        }
    }
)
```

The rest are exactly the same:

```
multi_worker_mirrored_strategy =
    tf.distribute.experimental.MultiWorkerMirroredStrategy()
```

```
with multi_worker_mirrored_strategy.scope():
    self.model = tf.keras.Model(inputs=inputs, outputs=x)
    self.model.compile(...)
    self.model.fit(...)
```

Central Storage Strategy

Another strategy that is worth mentioning, is the central storage strategy. This approach applies only to environments where we have a single machine with multiple GPUs. When our GPUs might not be able to store the entire model, we designate the CPU's memory as the main storage unit which holds the global state of the model. To this end, the variables are not mirrored into the different devices, but they are all kept in the CPU.

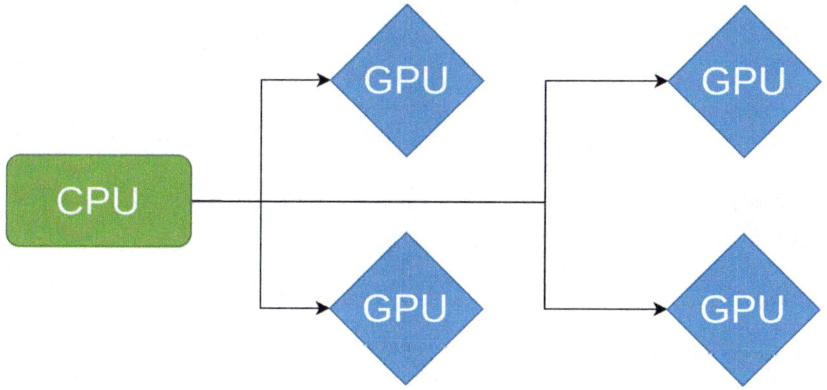

Figure 6.12: Central storage strategy

Therefore, the CPU sends the variables to the GPUs which perform the training, compute the gradients, update the weights, and send them back to the CPU. They are then combined using a reduce operation.

```
central_storage_strategy =
    tf.distribute.experimental.CentralStorageStrategy()
```

6.3.4 Asynchronous training

Synchronous training has a lot of advantages, but it can be hard to scale. Furthermore, it may result in the workers staying idle for a long time. If the workers differ on capability, are down for maintenance, or have different priorities, then **an async approach might be a better choice because workers won't wait on each other**.

A good rule of thumb, which is applicable in most cases, is:

- If we have many small, unreliable and limited-capability devices, it's better to use an async approach.
- If, on the other hand, we have strong devices with powerful communication links, a synchronous approach might be the better choice.

Now, let's clarify in simple terms how async training works.

The difference from sync training is that the workers are executing the training of the model into different rates and each one of them does not need to wait for the others. But how do we accomplish that?

Parameter Server Strategy

The most dominant technique is called Parameter Server Strategy. When having a cluster of workers, we can assign a different role to each one. In other words, we designate some devices to act as parameter servers and some devices as training workers.

Parameter servers: They hold the parameters of our model and are responsible for updating them (global state of our model).

Training workers: They run the actual training loop and produce the gradients and the loss from the data.

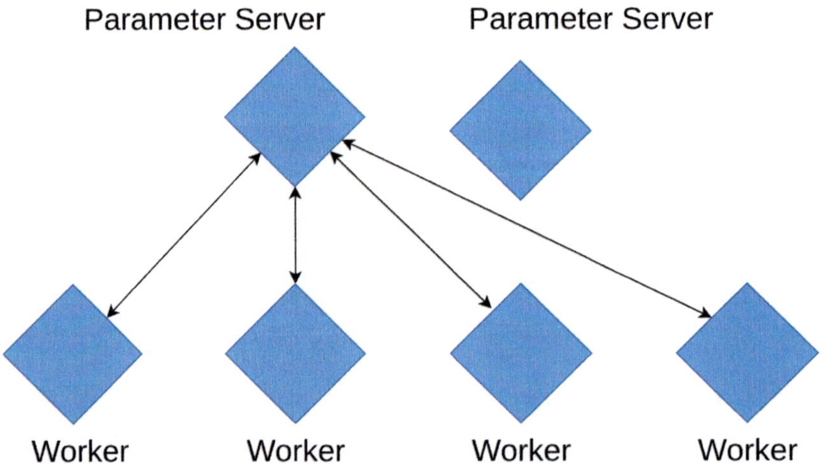

Figure 6.13: Parameter server strategy

So here is the complete flow:

1. We again replicate the model in all our workers.
2. Each training worker fetches the parameters from the parameter servers.
3. It performs a training loop.
4. Once the worker is done, it sends the gradients back to all the parameter servers which update the model weights.

As you may be able to tell, this allows us to run the training independently in each worker and scale it across many of them. In Tensorflow it looks something like this:

```
ps_strategy = tf.distribute.experimental.ParameterServerStrategy()
parameter_server_strategy =
    tf.distribute.experimental.ParameterServerStrategy()

os.environ["TF_CONFIG"] = json.dumps(
    {
        "cluster": {
            "worker": ["host1:port", "host2:port", "host3:port"],
            "ps":  ["host4:port", "host5:port"]
        },
        "task": {
            "type": "worker",
            "index": 1
        }
    }
)
```

6.3.5 Model parallelism

So far, we talked about how to distribute our data and train the model in multiple devices with different data chunks. However, can we split the model architecture instead of the data? Actually, that's exactly what model parallelism is. Even though it is harder to implement, it's definitely worth mentioning.

When a model is so big that it **doesn't fit in the memory of a single device**, we can divide it into different parts, distribute them across multiple machines, and train each independently using the same data.

An intuitive example might be to train each layer of a neural network in a different device. Or perhaps in an encoder-decoder architecture, to train the decoder and the encoder into different machines.

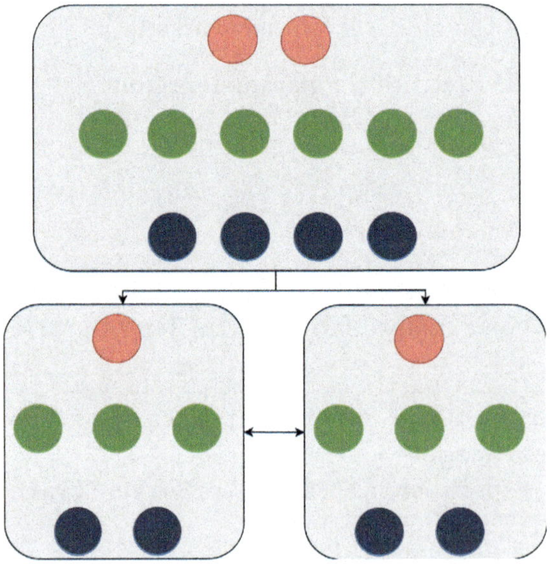

Figure 6.14: Model parallelism

Although, keep in mind that in the majority of cases the GPU has enough memory to fit their entire model. Let's examine a simple example to make that perfectly clear. Imagine that we have a small neural network with an input layer, a hidden layer, and an output layer.

The hidden layer consists of 6 nodes. A good way to parallelize our model would be to train the first 3 nodes of the hidden layer into one machine and the next 3 nodes into a different machine. Yeah, I know that is an absolute overkill but for example's sake let's discuss the overall flow:

1. We feed the exact same batch of data into both machines.
2. We train each part of the model separately.
3. We combine the actual gradients using an all-reduce approach as in data parallelism.
4. We run the backward pass of the backpropagation algorithm in both machines.
5. And finally, we update the weights based on the aggregated gradients.

Notice that the first machine will update only the first half of the weights while the second machine the second half.

As I have already mentioned, the most common use case of model parallelism is natural language processing models such as Transformers, GPT, BERT etc. In fact, in some applications, engineers **combine data parallelism and model parallelism to train those models as fast and as efficiently as possible**.

Which reminds me that there is a Tensorflow library that tries to alleviate the pain of splitting models called `Tensorflow Mesh`. If you are interested in model parallelism training, this is where you should start.

Chapter 7

Serving

In this chapter:

- How to create a deep learning application with Flask
- How to utilize load balancers such as Nginx
- How to take advantage of model servers

Developing and designing a state-of-the-art deep learning model has no real value if it can't be served as a real-world application. Don't get me wrong, research is awesome. However, most of the time the end goal is to solve a real-life problem. In the case of ML models, a big majority of them are actually deployed in a web or mobile application. In this chapter, **we will take our image segmentation model, build a web application on top of it and expose it in the web, via an API (Application Programming Interface), to the end users**.

7.1 Preparing the model

Ideally, we would like to provide a service that can be called by users and perform segmentation on custom images in real time. This technically translates to a client-server application. You don't need to be already familiar with this terminology. We will start by explaining a set of terms that will be used heavily throughout this chapter.

Glossary for client-server applications:

- **Web service**: any self-contained piece of software that makes itself available over the Internet and uses a standard communication protocol such as HTTP.
- **Server**: a computer program or device that provides a service to another computer program and its user, also known as the client.
- **Client-server**: a programming model in which one program (the client) requests a service or resource from another program (the server).
- **API**: a set of definitions and functions that allows applications to access data and interact with external software components, operating systems, or microservices.

So, let's pause for a moment and think what we want to do. We first need to have some sort of predictor (or `Inferrer`) class. In simple terms, an `Inferrer` will interact with our Tensorflow model to compute a segmentation map. Then, we need to build a **web application** to expose that functionality (API). Finally, we need to create a **web service** that allows clients to send their own images for prediction.

7.1.1 Building the model's inference function

Recap: We have trained the model using a custom training loop and then we saved the training variables using the Tensorflow built-in saving functionality.

```
save_path = os.path.join(self.model_save_path, "unet")
tf.saved_model.save(self.model, save_path)
```

Our next steps in a nutshell: a) load the saved model, b) feed it with the user's image, and c) infer the segmentation mask.

A good way to do that is to build an `Inferrer` class. The latter will load the model on creation (to avoid loading it multiple times). It will have an `infer` method that returns the segmentation mask. Don't forget that the user's image might not be in our desired format. To this end, we need to do some image pre-processing before we feed it to the model.

```
class UnetInferrer:
    def __init__(self):
        self.saved_path = 'model_path_location'
        self.model = tf.saved_model.load(self.saved_path)
        self.predict = self.model.signatures["serving_default"]
```

Notably, Tensorflow uses a saved model format that is optimized for serving the model in a web service. Because of the way the model is saved, we can't simply load it and perform a `keras.predict()`. The object that we use to represent a saved model contains a set of specific fields. In more detail, it has different graph metadata (called tag constants) and a set of fields that define the different input, output, and method names (called signature constants). Moreover, most of saved models, have a `serving_default` key, which represents a forward pass.

For that reason, we need to get the value from the signature and define a `predict` function ourselves. To perform a prediction on an image, we can do something like this:

```
prediction= self.predict(input image)['conv2d_transpose_4]
```

In our example, the output layer name is `conv2d_transpose_4`. In general, a good practice is to define custom names for the layers and the variables.

To continue, let's define a pre-process method. We only need to resize the image and normalize it to [0,1].

```
def preprocess(self, image):
        image = tf.image.resize(
            image,
            (self.image_size, self.image_size)
        )
        return tf.cast(image, tf.float32) / 255.0
```

Finally, we need an `infer` method that encapsulates the entire functionality. It takes an image as an argument and returns the segmentation output. Note that the image won't be in a `tf.Tensor` format. So, we first need to convert it, then apply the pre-processing step and finally perform the actual prediction.

```
def infer(self, image=None):
        tensor_image = tf.convert_to_tensor(image, dtype=tf.float32)
        tensor_image = self.preprocess(tensor_image)
        shape= tensor_image.shape
        tensor_image = tf.reshape(
             tensor_image,[1, shape[0],shape[1], shape[2]]
        )
        return self.predict(tensor_image)['conv2d_transpose_4']
```

Did you notice the extra step here? In general, the images are 3-dimensional tensors (channels, height, width) but the model expects a 4-dimensional tensor. To ensure that the input is in the correct format, we need to reshape the images.

To be absolutely sure that our method is correct, we may want to implement a very simple but incredibly useful unit test.

```python
from PIL import Image
import numpy as np
from executor.unet_inferrer import UnetInferrer

class MyTestCase(unittest.TestCase):

    def test_infer(self):
        image = np.asarray(
            Image.open('resources/yorkshire_terrier.jpg')
        ).astype(np.float32)
        inferrer = UnetInferrer()
        inferrer.infer(image)
```

Briefly, we load a simple image with a cute Yorkshire terrier, convert it to a Numpy array and use our `infer` function to make sure that everything works as expected.

We are ready to continue with creating our **web server with Flask**. As we will see, this is not very accurate since Flask is not a web server.

7.2 Creating a web application using Flask

7.2.1 Basics of modern web applications

In the client-server paradigm, the client sends a request to the server, the server processes that request by executing a piece of software and returns a response back to the client. This simple sentence raises the following questions.

How does the client know in what format the server expects the request (data)?

This is taken care of by the HTTP protocol. HTTP defines the communication between a server and a client. It also instructs how messages are formatted and transmitted, and what action the server and the client need to take in response to various commands and request types.

What does an HTTP request look like?

An HTTP request has 4 basic components: a destination URL, a method, some metadata called headers, and optionally a request body.

- The destination URL is a remote path under which the server functionality lives. From the server's perspective, this is called a route and it includes a URL plus a specific port.
- A method is the type of the request. In HTTP we have four basic types: GET, POST, UPDATE, DELETE. Depending on the method, the server will expose a different functionality under the hood.
- Headers are various metadata such as date, status, content type, and other stuff that are necessary for the client and server to interact.
- The Body contains the full data that we send over the web. This component is optional.

Note that an HTTP response has the exact same format.

How does the client know where to send the request?

The URL alongside the method defines an endpoint, which is a specific point of entry on a server.

```
Route: localhost:8080/semantic-segmentation
Method: POST
Endpoint: POST localhost:8080/semantic-segmentation
```

Different methods with the same route define different endpoints and therefore different functionalities.

How do we actually communicate with the server?

To communicate with the server all we need to do is send a POST request to specific URL (e.g. `localhost:8080/semantic-segmentation`).

These are the absolute necessary things to know in order to build our web application.

7.2.2 Exposing the deep learning model using Flask

A vital question first. What is Flask?

Flask is a web application framework that enables us to build simple applications with minimal boilerplate code and a few out of the box functionalities. Flask is built on top of the WSGI (web server gateway interface) protocol. WSGI is a protocol written in Python that describes how a web server communicates with web applications and is a part of Python's standard library (more on WSGI on the next section).

However, **Flask is not a fully functional web server and should not be used for production use**. A better approach might be something like the uWSGI web server that we will explore later. It's a perfect solution though to develop a quick app and do some prototyping on how our web server will look like.

Flask, like all the other web frameworks, provides some basic features:

- It helps us define different routes based on a URL, so we can expose different functionalities.
- It exposes different endpoints via different HTTP methods.
- It comes with some nice-to-have extras like integrated support for unit testing, built-in server, debugger and HTML templating.

The first thing we need to do in order to create an app, is to import Flask and create a new instance of it.

```
from flask import Flask, request
app = Flask(__name__)
```

To start the application, we can use the `run()` method on a form like:

```
HOST= 0.0.0.0
PORT_NUBER=8080

if __name__ == '__main__':
    app.run(host=HOST, port=PORT_NUMBER)
```

The `HOST` is our URL (in our case localhost) and the `PORT_NUMBER` is the standard 8080.

Now, we want to build our endpoint on a specific route. For example, we can have `0.0.0.0:8080/infer` as our endpoint and use a `POST` method.

Best practice: If we don't want to hard-code the URL and make it flexible for different environments, we can get the `APP_ROOT` environmental variable from OS and append the `/infer` path.

```
APP_ROOT = os.getenv('APP_ROOT', '/infer')
```

We also want to create an instance of our `Inferrer` class outside of the endpoint, so we don't have to load the model on each request.

```
u_net = UnetInferrer()
```

And our endpoint will finally look like this:

```
@app.route(APP_ROOT, methods=["POST"])
def infer():
    data = request.json
    image = data['image']
    return u_net.infer(image)
```

Let's examine that more carefully. The `app.route` decorator accepts the URL and the method. It lets Flask know that we will expose a particular functionality in this endpoint. For other endpoints you might want to create, you can follow the exact same pattern.

The request object is built-in inside Flask and it contains a full HTTP request with all the things mentioned before. The request body is in json format by default, so we can easily get the image and feed it into our `Inferrer` class. Every time a user wants to predict a segmentation mask of an image, all they have to do is send an HTTP request to that specific endpoint.

Another cool feature that Flask has, is a very intuitive way to handle all the exceptions that might occur during the execution of our app.

```
from flask import jsonify
@app.errorhandler(Exception)
def handle_exception(e):
    return jsonify(stackTrace=traceback.format_exc())
```

This will be triggered every time an error happens, and it will return a traceback of the failed Python code to the console. Of course, Flask has more features, but we focus on the principles rather than the tool. In real-life projects, you will often need to spend some time checking the official docs of the tool for more features.

Great, our server is up and running. However, can we be sure that everything works perfectly? There is only one way to find out: testing it! We need to build a simple client to send an HTTP request and examine the response. An even more ideal approach would be to create a simple UI on the browser, but that goes out of the scope of this book. The advantage of building an actual UI is that we can plot the resulting segmentation and test everything.

Creating a client to test the endpoint can be thought of as an acceptance test, which will validate the functionality of our entire application. We can run the acceptance test before every deployment to make sure that we won't push buggy code in production.

7.2.3 Creating a client

Our client will be nothing more than a Python script that sends a request and displays the response. Python has an amazing library called `requests` that makes sending and receiving HTTP requests quite straightforward. Our client script will load an image from a local folder and then we will create an HTTP request and send it to the server.

```
import requests
from PIL import Image
import numpy as np
ENDPOINT_URL = http://0.0.0.0:8080/infer

def infer():
    image = np.asarray(
        Image.open('resources/yorkshire_terrier.jpg')
    ).astype(np.float32)
    data = { 'image': image.tolist() }
    response = requests.post(ENDPOINT_URL, json = data)
    response.raise_for_status()
    print(response)
```

After loading the image and converting it to a Numpy array, we create a json object called `data`, do a POST request to our endpoint URL, and print the response. An alternative will be to have an `assert` method here, which would automatically check the generated mask.

Because HTTP doesn't recognize Numpy arrays or Tensorflow tensors, we have to convert the image into a list (which is a json compatible object). This also means that our response will contain a list.

The command `response.raise_for_status()` is a little trick that will raise an exception if the server returns an error. That way, we can be sure that the rest of our program won't continue with a falsified response.

Since printing a 3-dimensional tensor is practically unreadable, let's instead plot the predicted image.

```
import matplotlib.pyplot as plt
import tensorflow as tf

def display(display_list):
    plt.figure(figsize=(15, 15))
    title = ['Input Image', 'Predicted Mask']
```

```
    for i in range(len(display_list)):
        plt.subplot(1, len(display_list), i + 1)
        plt.title(title[i])
        plt.imshow(
            tf.keras.preprocessing.image.
                array_to_img(display_list[i])
        )
        plt.axis('off')
    plt.show()
```

And there we have it. The segmentation mask of a Yorkshire terrier as shown in the Figure 7.1.

Figure 7.1: Image segmentation on a pet image

Eventually, everything works fine. Both our server and client do what they are supposed to do. I don't know if you realized it, but we just created the first version of our web application. A deep learning-powered app. How cool is that?

Unfortunately, we're not done yet. At the moment, our web server runs only locally, it is using Flask which is not optimized for production environments, and it can't handle many users at the same time.

7.3 Serving with uWSGI and Nginx

In this section, we will discover how to utilize uWSGI to create a high-performance production-ready server and how to use a load balancer like Nginx to distribute the traffic equally to multiple processes. We will explore step by step how to start from the Flask prototype we built, wire up uWSGI to act as a full web server, and hide it behind Nginx to provide a more robust connection handling. As a result, we will be able to serve lots of users at the same time.

7.3.1 Basic Terminology

Before we dive into the components of our application, we will present some definitions. That way, you will be able to understand the differences between them. The 2 main systems we'll use besides Flask are: a) uWSGI b) Nginx.

What is uWSGI?

According to the official website, uWSGI is an application server that aims to provide a full-stack solution for developing and deploying web applications and services.

Like most application servers, it is language-agnostic, meaning that is independent of the programming language. However, its most popular use is for serving Python applications. uWSGI is built on top of the WSGI (Web Server Gateway Interface) specification. It communicates with the other servers over a low-level protocol called uwsgi. Because this is very confusing, we need to clarify some things up, so let's start with some definitions.

- **WSGI** (Web Server Gateway Interface): defines the communication between a web server and a web application. In simple terms, it tells us what methods should be implemented to pass requests and responses back and forth between the server and the application. You can think of it as an API interface that's being used to standardize communication and is part of Python's standard library.
- **uWSGI**: An application server that communicates with the application based on the WSGI spec, and with other web servers over a variety of other protocols (such as HTTP). Most of the times, it acts like a middleware because it translates requests from a conventional web server into a format that the application understands (WSGI).
- **uwsgi**: A low-level/binary protocol that enables communication between web servers. uwsgi is a wire protocol that has been implemented by the uWSGI server as the preferred way to speak with other web servers and uWSGI instances. So, in essence it defines the format of the data sent between servers and instances.

Why do we need uWSGI? Isn't Flask adequate?

While Flask can act as an HTTP web server, it was simply not developed for that. It's not optimized as one in terms of security, scalability, and efficiency. It is rather a framework to build web applications. uWSGI on the other hand, was created as a fully functional web server and it solves many problems out of the box that Flask doesn't even touch.

Examples are:

- **Process management**: it handles the creation and maintenance of multiple processes so we can have a concurrent app in a single environment and is able to scale to multiple users.
- **Clustering**: it can be used in a cluster of instances.
- **Load balancing**: it balances the load of requests to different processes
- **Monitoring**: it provides out of the box functionality to monitor the performance and resource utilization.
- **Resource limiting**: it can be configured to limit the CPU and memory usage up to a specific point.
- **Configuration**: it has a huge variety of configurable options that gives us full control over its execution.

Having said that, let's inspect our next tool: Nginx.

What is Nginx?

Nginx is a high performance, highly scalable, and highly available web server. It can act as a **load balancer**, a **reverse proxy**, and a **caching mechanism**. It can also be used to serve static files, to provide security and encryption on the requests, to rate-limit them, and it supposedly can handle more than 10,000 simultaneous connections. It is basically uWSGI on steroids.

Nginx is extremely popular and is a part of many big companies' tech stack. So why should we use it in front of uWSGI? Well, the main reason is that we simply want the best of both worlds. We want those uWSGI features that are Python-specific but we also like all the extra functionalities Nginx provides. Again, we expect our application to be scaled to thousands of users. Plus, it's a useful knowledge to have as a ML engineer. No one expects us to be experts but knowing the fundamentals can't really hurt us.

Note that uWSGI can definitely be used on its own without Nginx and it even might be a better approach for many smaller projects.

Nginx as a reverse proxy: what is a reverse proxy and why use it?

A reverse proxy is simply a system that forwards all requests from the web to our web server and back. It is a single point of communication with the outer world and it comes with some incredibly useful features. First of all, it can balance the load of million requests and distribute the traffic evenly in many uWSGI instances. Secondly it provides a level of security that can prevent attacks and uses encryption in communications. Last but not least, it can also cache content and responses that speed up performance.

What is a web socket?

Nginx usually communicates with other internal systems using a web socket. A web socket is a bidirectional secure connection that enables a two-way interactive communication session between a user and a client. By using sockets, we can send messages to a server and receive event-driven responses without having to poll the server for a reply.

7.3.2 Designing a serving system

Now that you have a clear image of the different components and their strengths, let's look at the whole picture. When designing our system, we need to make sure that everything ties together correctly. The overall flow of data will be as shown below:

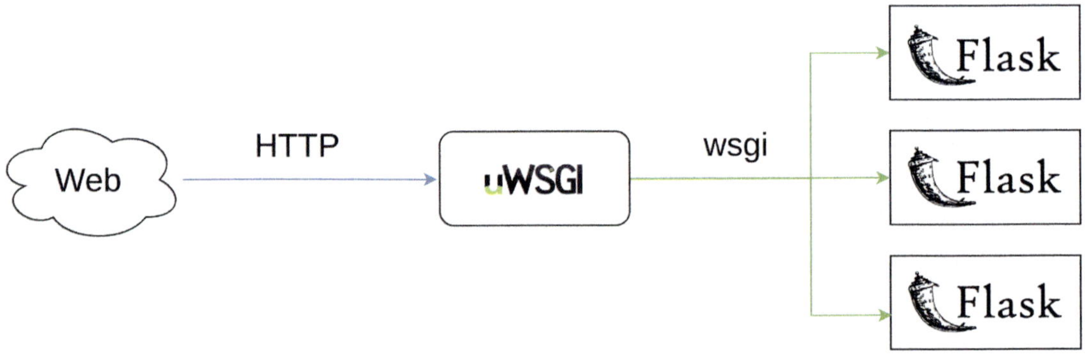

Figure 7.2: Flow of data in a Flask-uWSGI application

- We have our software exposed to a web app using Flask.
- The application will be served using the uWSGI server and it will communicate with it using the WSGI spec.

- The uWSGI server now will be hidden behind another web server (Nginx) with whom it will communicate using the uwsgi protocol.

uWSGI will be responsible for executing the Flask application with the Tensorflow model and providing the segmentation. Nginx will be used as a reverse proxy in front of uWSGI, with whom it will communicate through a web socket. Nginx will handle the load balancing and will act as a single point of communication with the outer world.

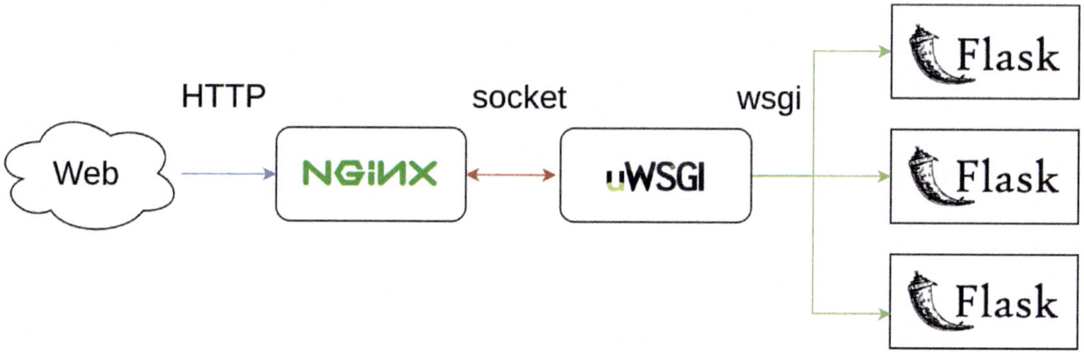

Figure 7.3: Flow of data in a Flask-uWSGI-Nginx application

Ok, enough with the theory. It's time to get our hands dirty and see how all these technologies can be configured and wired up in practice.

7.3.3 Setting up a uWSGI server with Flask

Here is a quick reminder of our Flask application as defined in the `service.py` file. It receives an image as a request, predicts its segmentation mask using the Tensorflow UNet model we built, and returns it to the client.

```
import os
import traceback
from flask import Flask, jsonify, request
from executor.unet_inferrer import UnetInferrer

app = Flask(__name__)

APP_ROOT = os.getenv('APP_ROOT', '/infer')
HOST = "0.0.0.0"
PORT_NUMBER = int(os.getenv('PORT_NUMBER', 8080))

u_net = UnetInferrer()
```

```
@app.route(APP_ROOT, methods=["POST"])
def infer():
    data = request.json
    image = data['image']
    return u_net.infer(image)

@app.errorhandler(Exception)
def handle_exception(e):
    return jsonify(stackTrace=traceback.format_exc())

if __name__ == '__main__':
    app.run(host=HOST, port=PORT_NUMBER)
```

The above code will remain intact. In order to utilize uWSGI, we just need to execute a few small steps on top of the Flask application.

After installing uWSGI with pip,

```
$ pip install uwsgi
```

we can spin up an instance with the following command:

```
$ uwsgi --http 0.0.0.0:8080  --wsgi-file service.py --callable app
```

This tells uWSGI to run a server in 0.0.0.0 and port 8080, using the application located in the `service.py` file, which is where our Flask code lives. We also need to provide a `callable` parameter that must be a function that can be called using the WSGI spec. In our case, it is the Flask instance we created in the `service.py` file and bound all the routes to.

```
app = Flask(__name__)
```

Tip: Note that instead of passing all the parameters using the command line, we can create a config file and make the server read directly from it. This is usually the preferred way especially because we will later deploy the server in the cloud. Admittedly, it is much easier to change a config option compared to altering a terminal command.

Analysing the uwsgi config file

A sample config file (`app.ini`) can look like this:

```
[uwsgi]

http = 0.0.0.0:8080
module = app.service
callable = app
die-on-term = true
chdir = /home/aisummer/src/soft_eng_for_dl/
virtualenv = /home/aisummer/miniconda3/envs
  /Deep-Learning-Production-Course/
processes = 1
master = false
vacuum = true
```

We declare our `http` url and `callable` as before, and we use the `module` option to indicate where the Python module containing our app is located. Apart from that, we need to specify some other things to avoid misconfigure the server such as the full directory path of the application (`chdir`) as well as the virtual environment path (if we use one).

Figure 7.4: Image segmentation of a pet image

Also notice that we don't use multiprocessing here (`process=1`) and we have a master process. `die-on-term` is a handy option that enables us to kill the server from the terminal, and `vacuum` dictates uWSGI to clean unused generated files periodically.

Configuring a uWSGI server is not straightforward and needs to be carefully examined because there are so many options and so many parameters to take into consideration. The best practice as an ML Engineer is to refer to the official docs and adjust the options that serve you best.

To execute the server, we can use the config file we created and run the following command:

```
$ uwsgi app.ini
```

We once again run the client script and we receive the segmentation mask as shown in the Figure 7.4.

7.3.4 Setting up Nginx as a reverse proxy

The next task in the to-do list is to set up the Nginx server which again is as simple as building a config file.

First, we install it using `apt-get install`:

```
$ sudo apt-get install nginx
```

Next, we want to create the config file that must live inside the "/etc/nginx/sites-available" directory (if you are on Linux) and has to be named after our application.

```
$ sudo nano /etc/nginx/sites-available/service.conf
```

Then, we create a very simple configuration file, called `service.conf`, that contains only the absolute minimum to run the proxy. Again, to discover all the available configuration options, be sure to check out the official documentation.

```
server {
    listen 80;
    server_name 0.0.0.0;

    location / {
        include       uwsgi_params;
        uwsgi_pass    unix:/home/aisummer/src/Deep_Learning-in-
                          Production/app/service.sock;
```

```
    }
}
```

Here we tell Nginx to listen to the default port 80 in localhost (0.0.0.0). The location block is identifying all requests coming from the web to the uWSGI server. This is done by including in the config the `uwsgi_params` term which specify all the generic uWSGI parameters, and the `uwsgi_pass` term which indicates uWSGI to forward them to the defined socket.

By now, you will realize that we haven't created a socket. That's right. That's why we need to declare the socket by adding the following 2 lines in our uWSGI config file:

```
socket = service.sock
chmod-socket = 660
```

This instructs the server to listen on the 660 socket using the uwsgi protocol.

At last, we enable the above configuration by running the below command that links our config in the `sites-available` directory with the `sites-enabled` directory.

```
$ sudo ln -s /etc/nginx/sites-available/service
    /etc/nginx/sites-enabled
```

Now we are ready to initiate Nginx:

```
$ sudo nginx -t
```

If everything went well, we should see our app in the localhost, and we can use a client once again to verify that everything works as expected.

All incoming requests will be routed from Nginx to the appropriate uWSGI instance, which will run the Flask application with our Tensorflow model. The response will be sent back to the client. And that's all. We just created a fully-functional, highly scalable web application powered by a deep learning model.

7.4 Serving with model servers

A very popular alternative way to deploy ML models is model servers. Model servers aim to simplify the deployment of ML at scale, provide quick iteration and reduce the friction between the research team and the DevOps team. That's why we will open a small parenthesis here and discuss more about model servers before proceeding with the deployment of our application.

The most notable example of a model server is Tensorflow serving (`tf.serving`). Tensorflow Serving is a high-performance serving system for machine learning models, designed for production environments.

Before we continue, we will clarify the differences between a conventional server like Flask and a model server like Tensorflow Serving.

7.4.1 Tensorflow Serving vs Flask

Well, for starters Flask has not been built as a production-ready server. Besides, model servers offer a few nice things on top of vanilla servers and are much more focused on ML applications. Here is a comparison table between Flask and Tensorflow Serving:

Flask	Tensorflow Serving
No consistency between APIs	Highly scalable
No model versioning	Consistent model export
No consistent payloads	Customized docker images
No mini-batch support	Inference via GRPC or REST endpoints
Different patterns/setups per mode	Model discovery
	Model A/B testing
	Batch inferences
	Highly customizable

So, let's start by exporting our trained model.

7.4.2 Export a Tensorflow model

To be able to load our model into the model server, it needs to be exported in a `protobuf` format. That way we have a consistent, highly optimized format for all our models.

Protocol buffers (protobuf) are Google's language-neutral, platform-neutral, extensible mechanism for serializing structured data.

Luckily Tensorflow makes that extremely easy using a simple command:

```
import tensorflow as tf

tf.saved_model.save( model, export_dir = save_path)
```

Note that the export folder can also contain things like external assets, Tensorflow variables that we want to save, or training checkpoints.

7.4.3 Install Tensorflow Serving

There are different ways to install Tensorflow Serving, but the easier one is using Docker. Not only does it play along very well with GPUs, but it is also dead simple.

Important note: I know that we haven't talked about Docker yet as we will analyse it extensively in the next chapter. For now, imagine Docker as a self-contained system that includes our application. The reason I included this section here, is to give you an overview of how easy it is to use model servers. All mentioned commands will be discussed extensively on Chapter 8. For now, I suggest to focus more on what we can do with model servers rather than how we do it. Once you understand Docker, the below code snippets will become trivial.

As with every Docker container, first, we need to pull the docker image from the Docker Hub.

```
$ docker pull tensorflow/serving
```

Once the image is pulled, we can execute our model server and open the REST API with a single command.

```
$ docker run -p 8501:8501 \
--mount type=bind, source=/path/to/saved_models, target=/models \
-e MODEL_NAME=unet \
-t tensorflow/serving &
```

The above command runs a Docker container using the `tensorflow/serving` image and opens the port 8500. It mounts inside the container the folder `saved_models`, which contains all our models, the folder `/models/models`. It also specifies which exact model the container should pick up.

Now we can send a request to the server using our client script and test the result:

```
import requests
from PIL import Image
import numpy as np

ENDPOINT_URL = "http://localhost:8501/models/unet:predict"
def infer():
    image = np.asarray(
        Image.open('resources/yorkshire_terrier.jpg')
    ).astype(np.float32)
```

```
    data ={'image': image.tolist()}
    response = requests.post(ENDPOINT_URL, json = data)
    response.raise_for_status()
    print(response.json())


if __name__ =="__main__":
    infer()
```

Notice that the ENDPOINT_URL corresponds to the API exposed by the model server.

7.4.4 Load a model

tf.serving enables you to load a model either from a local folder or a remote location. Assuming that we have stored our protobuf models in the cloud, say AWS S3 or Google Cloud Storage, we can easily use the remote models in our servers. Thus, instead of mounting a local folder in the container as we did before, we now point to the remote bucket.

```
$ docker run -p 8501:8501 \
-e MODEL_BASE_PATH=s3://bucketname/my_models_path/
-e MODEL_NAME=unet
-t tensorflow/serving &
```

7.4.5 Multiple versions support

In a similar way, we can also support multiple versions of the same model simultaneously. In this case, the server will expose two different endpoints for each version. This can be done using a config file. Be aware that the config needs to be a ModelServerConfig protocol buffer. Don't be scared by it. It is as simple as shown below:

```
model_config_list {
        config {
        name: my_model
        base_path: '/path_to_saved_models/my_model/'
        model_platform: 'tensorflow'
        model_version_policy {
            specific {
                versions: 42
                versions: 43
            }
```

```
        }
    }
}
```

The above config would require our base_path folder to contain two different sub-folders, named 42 and 43 in this case. Each sub-folder must have a protobuf model. To use the model config when initializing the container, we have the --model_config_file argument:

```
$ docker run -p 8501:8501 \
--mount type=bind, source=/path/to/saved_models,
    target=/models \
-e MODEL_NAME=unet
--mount type=bind, source=/path/to/model_config,
    target=/models/model_config
--model_config_file= /models/model_config
-t tensorflow/serving &
```

This functionality can be used to perform simple A/B testing between different versions of a model if you don't mind performing it client-side. However, notice that it is usually better to support this functionality on the server side.

7.4.6 Multiple models support

It is natural to question if a similar config can be used to serve entirely different models simultaneously. Of course, it can. All we have to do is specify the base path for each one of them and we are good to go:

```
model_config_list {
  config {
    name: 'my_first_model'
    base_path: '/path_to_saved_models/my_first_model/'
    model_platform: 'tensorflow'
  }
  config {
    name: 'my_second_model'
    base_path: '/path_to_saved_models/my_second_model/'
    model_platform: 'tensorflow'
  }
}
```

Nevertheless, serving non-identical models under the same container is not recommended for production environments. The reason is that we lose the ability to scale them in a different manner. Each model has its own scalability, memory, and processing needs.

7.4.7 Batching inferences

One of the features of `tf_sertving` I'm most excited about is batching inferences. It should be highlighted that batching inferences is natively supported by `tf.serving` contrary to Flask. Behind the scenes, the model server aggregates inference requests and executes them as a group.

To enable this functionality, we first need to set some ground rules. For example, what's the maximum batch size, how long the server should wait for aggregating a batch, etc. Once again, we will use a config file, which will look like this:

```
max_batch_size { value: 32}
batch_timeout_micros {value : 1000}
max_enqueued_batches { value: 1000000 }
num_batch_threads { value: 4 }
```

This effectively changes the `docker run` command as:

```
$ docker run -p 8501:8501 \
--mount type=bind, source=/path/to/saved_models, target=/models \
-e MODEL_NAME=unet
--mount type=bind, source=/path/to/model_config,
    target=/models/model_config
--model_config_file= /models/model_config
--mount type=bind, source=/path/to/batch_config,
    target=/models/batch_config
--enable_batching=true
--batching_parameters_file = /path/to/batch_config/
    batching_parameters.txt
-t tensorflow/serving
```

Model servers such as `tf.serving` have some important advantages compared to plain web servers. One should seriously consider incorporating them into their project. Nonetheless, they shouldn't be treated as panacea. The fact that they are very opinionated makes them unpractical for many problems and infrastructures. To conclude, whether you should choose model servers, uWSGI, Nginx or another alternative, depends heavily on the specific use case. In our image segmentation example, we will proceed without a model server since we will set up a Docker container ourselves.

Chapter 8

Deploying

In this chapter:

- How to use Docker
- How to containerize deep learning applications
- How to deploy your app into the cloud

It's finally time. Everything is in place for the model to be pushed into production. But how? This is the part most data scientists and ML researchers are less familiar with. Over the past years, containers have been the go-to solution to package an ML application. Without a doubt, this isn't the only option. Virtual machines and serverless applications also have their piece of the pie. However, containers and Docker have the lion's share in real-life scenarios.

In this chapter, we will containerize our deep learning application using Docker. First, we will explain some basic principles about containers and Docker, then we will build a Docker image that packages our deep learning/Flask/uWSGI code, an image for Nginx, and we will combine them using Docker Compose.

8.1 Containerizing using Docker and Docker Compose

Containers have become the standard way to develop and deploy applications these days. You have probably heard about Docker and Kubernetes. These tools have managed to dominate the ML field. Why? They provide flexibility to experiment with different frameworks, versions, GPUs, with minimal overhead. Besides that, they eliminate discrepancies between the development and the production environment, they are lightweight compared to virtual machines, and they can easily be scaled up or down.

8.1.1 What is a container?

A container is a standard unit of software that packages the code and all its dependencies, so the application runs quickly and reliably from one computing environment to another.

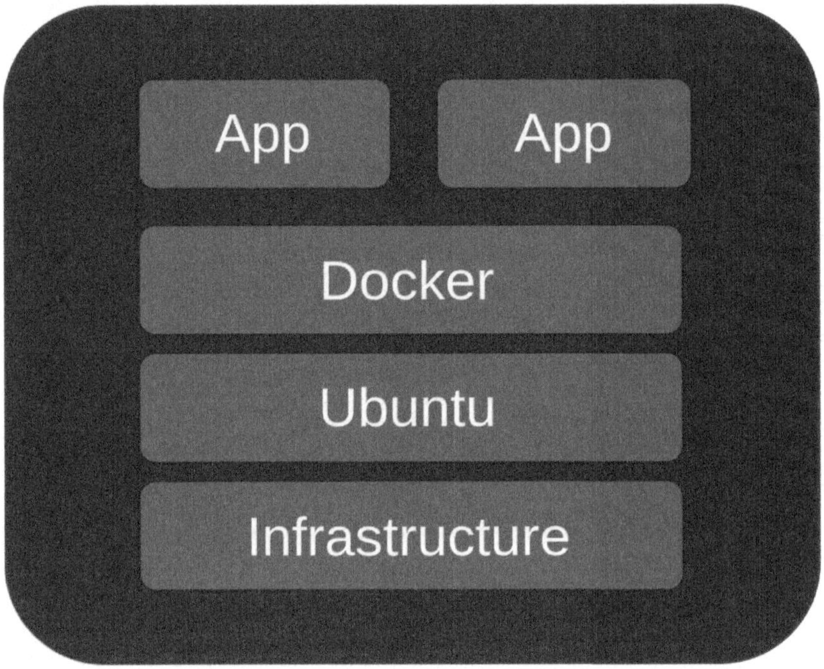

Figure 8.1: A containerized application

This means that we can run the exact same software in any environment regardless of the operating system and hardware. As you might have guessed, this immediately solves problems such as missing dependencies. Containers enable easy collaboration between developers, and they provide isolation from other applications. And of course, they eliminate a statement that originates from the beginning of time:

"It works on my machine; I don't understand why it doesn't work here."

Note that containers run on top of the operating system's kernel. As such, they are more lightweight and portable compared to virtual machines, which virtualize

Operating System (OS) images.

8.1.2 What is Docker

Docker has become so incredibly popular since 2013 that is essentially synonymous with containers. These two terms have been used indistinguishably. I was tempted to mention a few other options but honestly, there is no point.

Docker is an open-source platform-as-a-service for building, deploying and managing containerized applications.

Moreover, it comes with a very powerful Command Line Interface (CLI), a desktop User Interface (UI) for those that prefer a visual approach (Docker Desktop), and a collection of thousands of ready-to-use container images (Docker Hub).

Ok, let's start using Docker in our real-life example. It is easier to explore more of its advantages utilizing our hands-on use case.

8.1.3 Setting up Docker

The first thing we need to do is install the Docker engine in our machine. Because it is more than a simple `apt-get install` command, I strongly recommend checking the official Docker documentation.

If everything went well, you should be able to run an example container:

```
$ docker run ubuntu
```

`ubuntu` is a container image that includes a minimal ubuntu installation. With `docker run IMAGE`, we can spin up the container.

Docker image

A docker image is nothing more than a template that contains a set of instructions for creating a container. It includes the elements needed to run the application as a container such as code, config files, environment variables, libraries. If the image is deployed to a Docker environment, it can then be executed as a Docker container.

If we'd like to enter the container, we can run the exact same command with an `-it` argument.

```
$ docker run -it ubuntu
```

Once we've done that, a bash terminal that gives us access to the container appears. Here we can do whatever we want. We can install things, execute software, and almost everything we do in our local system. To exit the terminal, just type **exit**. Just to give you an example, let's inspect the folder structure of our container:

```
root@5bb91d6c145d:/# ls
bin  boot  dev  etc  home  lib  lib32  lib64  libx32  media  mnt  opt
    proc  root  run  sbin  srv  sys  tmp  usr  var
root@5bb91d6c145d:/#
```

To see all running containers, **docker ps** is the go-to command:

```
$ docker ps

# CONTAINER ID  IMAGE   COMMAND CREATED STATUS  PORTS   NAMES
# 5bb91d6c145d  ubuntu  "/bin/bash" 4 minutes ago   Up 4 minutes
```

Here is where the magic comes: the same container can be pulled from another environment or system and it will have the exact same software and dependencies.

8.1.4 Building a deep learning Docker image

It's time to build our Tensorflow-Flask-uWSGI image that contains our UNet model.

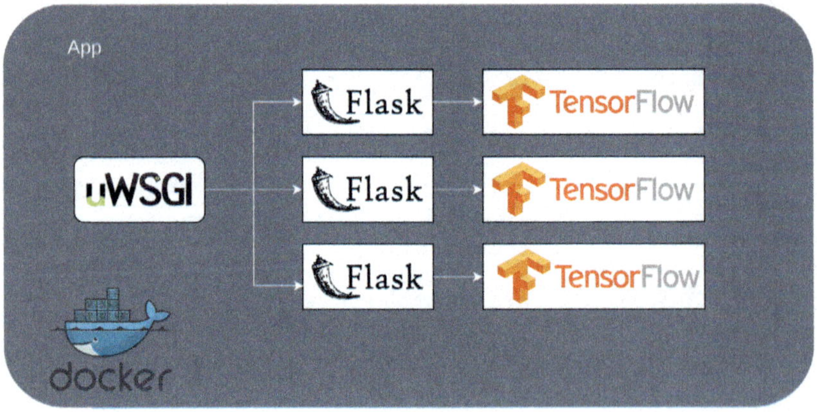

Figure 8.2: A Docker image of a Deep Learning application

To do so, we need to know what dependencies are necessary to include in the image. If you have been following along and are developing the whole app inside the virtual environment with only the essentials libraries, you can do:

```
$ pip freeze > requirements.txt
```

This command will take all the installed libraries inside the virtual environment and write them in a `requirements.txt` file alongside with their versions. A few hand-picked libraries inside the file are:

```
Flask==1.1.2
uWSGI==2.0.18
Tensorflow==2.2.0
```

Tip 1: An important detail to know here is that we probably don't need to declare all these libraries that `pip freeze` emitted because most of them are dependencies of other libraries. If I had to guess, I'd say that including the above three, would be sufficient but don't take my word for granted.

Tip 2: It is critical to include the library version in your `requirements.txt` file, since later versions of the modules may change the code's behaviour. This is a common source of errors that can be avoided.

In fact, we won't even need to include Tensorflow. That's because we will use an existing Tensorflow image from Docker Hub as our basis.

Restructuring our app for deployment

The next step is to restructure our application for deployment. The key principle here is that all the necessary code needed to run an inference should be included inside a single folder. This is due to the fact that we can't have the docker container reading from multiple folders and modules. Let's remind ourselves of our application first.

Our Flask app:

```python
import os
import traceback

from flask import Flask, jsonify, request
from unet_inferrer import UnetInferrer

app = Flask(__name__)

APP_ROOT = os.getenv('APP_ROOT', '/infer')
HOST = "0.0.0.0"
PORT_NUMBER = int(os.getenv('PORT_NUMBER', 8080))

u_net = UnetInferrer()
```

```
@app.route(APP_ROOT, methods=["POST"])
def infer():
    data = request.json
    image = data['image']
    return u_net.infer(image)
```

Apart from the UnetInferrer class, I don't see any other code dependencies, so let's include that one as well.

```
import tensorflow as tf

class UnetInferrer:
    def __init__(self):
        self.image_size = 128

        self.saved_path = 'unet'
        self.model = tf.saved_model.load(self.saved_path)

        self.predict = self.model.signatures["serving_default"]

    def preprocess(self, image):
        image = tf.image.resize(image,
            (self.image_size, self.image_size)
        )
        return tf.cast(image, tf.float32) / 255.0

    def infer(self, image=None):
        tensor_image = tf.convert_to_tensor(image, dtype=tf.float32)
        tensor_image = self.preprocess(tensor_image)
        shape= tensor_image.shape
        tensor_image = tf.reshape(
           tensor_image,[1, shape[0],shape[1], shape[2]]
        )
        pred = self.predict(tensor_image)['conv2d_transpose_4']
        pred = pred.numpy().tolist()
        return {'segmentation_output':pred}
```

Can you guess what did I forgot?

1. The trained model that we want to deploy, of course. To this end, we will include all the trained variables inside the folder as well.

2. The uWSGI config file.

So far, we have:

1. Our trained Tensorflow model
2. Our Flask application
3. Our uWSGI configuration
4. The `requirements.txt` file with all the dependencies

Now we are ready to move on. As you see below, the `app` folder contains all the necessary stuff for deployment.

```
app/
  unet/
  app.ini
  requirements.txt
  service.py
  unet_inferrer.py
```

Now that we have our `app` folder, it is time to write our Dockerfile.

Dockerfiles

Dockerfiles are contract files that provide all the necessary steps Docker needs to take while building an image. Inside them, we write a set of commands to specify how our Docker image will be. They can vary from having 5 lines of simple commands to hundreds. Another great thing about Dockerfiles is that Docker won't execute the whole sequence every time. Once the Docker image is built, on any subsequent execution it will run only the commands below the line that changed. Therefore, we can experiment with different libraries, while not having to wait every time for the entire image to get built.

So, let's open an empty text file and start building our Dockerfile. Note that Dockerfiles don't have a specific file extension; they should simply be named as `Dockerfile`.

A good practice to follow: every Docker image should be built on top of another image. The latter can be a very primitive image such us `ubuntu` with only the OS kernel and basic libraries, or a high-level one like `tensorflow` which is the one we will use here.

```
FROM tensorflow/tensorflow:2.0.0
```

Tensorflow provides a variety of images for different versions and different environments (CPU vs GPU). `tensorflow` is the name of the image while `2.0.0` is the tag. Tags are used to differentiate images from the same vendor.

Alternatively, we could use a basic Linux image and install all the dependencies ourselves. However, this is suboptimal and usually avoided because the official images are highly optimized in terms of memory consumption and build time.

Let's inspect our Dockerfile commands line by line:

```
WORKDIR /app
```

The `WORKDIR` line sets the working directory inside the container into the `/app` folder, so that any commands or code executions will happen there. And of course, we need to add our local folder inside the container. This is required because the docker container is self-contained and does not have access to our local file system.

```
ADD . /app
```

Now, all our files are now present inside the container so we should be able to install all the required Python libraries.

```
RUN pip install -r requirements.txt
```

Did you notice that we haven't installed Python so far? The reason behind that, is that the `tensorflow` image contains Python3, pip, and other necessary libraries. To have a peek inside the image, you can visit the Docker Hub website.

Finally, as everything is in place, we can initiate the uWSGI server with the `CMD` command. The `CMD` command will not be invoked during build-time but during run-time.

```
CMD ["uwsgi", "app.ini"]
```

Writing Dockerfiles is not always as straightforward as you might imagine, so I would recommend spending some time going through the documentation.

If we haven't missed anything, we can now build the image and instruct Docker to execute all these steps in order. I will name the image `deep-learning-production` and give it a `1.0` tag to differentiate it from future versions.

```
$ docker build -t deep-learning-production:1.0 .
```

Be aware that this may take a while, because the `tensorflow` image is quite big. If everything went fine, we should see the following output.

```
Successfully built SOME_RANDOM_ID
Successfully tagged deep-learning-production:1.0
```

8.1.5 Running a deep learning docker container

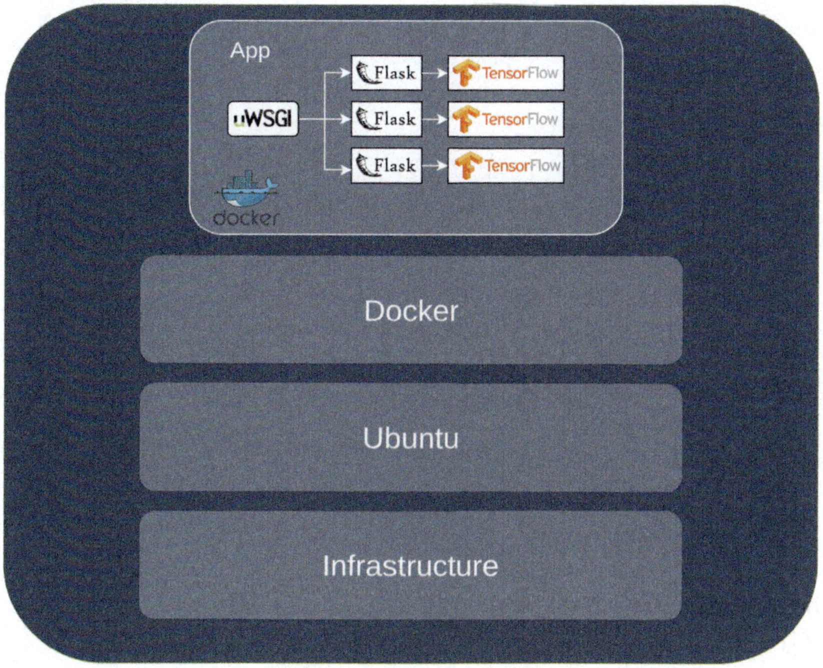

Figure 8.3: A containerized Deep Learning application

It's time to run our container and fire up our server inside of it.

```
$ docker run --publish 80:8080  --name dlp
    deep-learning-production:1.0
```

Two things to highlight here:

- The `publish` argument will expose the 8080 port of the container to the 80 port of our local system, which means that every request coming to `localhost:80` will be routed to 8080 inside the container. This can be regarded as a communication between our local system and the Docker container. Always remember that the Docker container is independent from our local system. Finally note that 8080 is the uWSGI listening port.

- A good practice is to also specify a name when running a container. Otherwise, we would have to use the random ID produced by Docker to refer to the container, and this can be quite cumbersome.

If the container was executed successfully, we will see logs of spawned uWSGI workers. Once again, we can test our system by running the client and sending an image to the server for inference.

To sum up, instead of running the server locally, we have developed a container that:

- includes all the necessary dependencies.
- is fully isolated from the rest of our system.
- can be moved intact to another machine or deployed in the cloud.

I hope that by now you see the flexibility and the simplicity containers provide.

To transport the container to another machine, we can either push the container to the Docker Hub so that other people can pull from it, or we can simply pass the Dockerfile and let the other developer build the image. Now we can be sure that everything will run on any machine.

8.1.6 Creating an Nginx container

Following the same principles, we can build the Nginx container, which will act in front of the uWSGI server, as a reverse proxy. Again, we must move all the files inside a single folder (in this case it is only the Nginx config), construct the Dockerfile, build and run the image.

The Nginx config (`nginx.conf`) has the below structure:

```
server {
    listen 80;

    location / {
        include   uwsgi_params;
        uwsgi_pass  app:660;
    }
}
```

The config essentially tells us that the Nginx server will listen on port 80, and route all the outside requests to the uWSGI server (app) in port 660 via the uwsgi protocol. Remember that in the uWSGI config file (app.ini), we had to change the listening port from the HTTP port 8080 to a socket port (660) in order to make it work with Nginx.

Our `app.ini` will then be transformed into:

```
[uwsgi]

module = service
socket = :660
callable = app
die-on-term = true
processes = 1
master = false
vacuum = true
```

The Nginx Dockerfile (see below) is quite simple because it does only two things. It pulls the original Nginx image and replaces the default configuration file with our custom one.

```
FROM nginx

RUN rm /etc/nginx/conf.d/default.conf
COPY nginx.conf /etc/nginx/conf.d/
```

The next step is, as always, to test our Nginx container. This time there is no point in running the container on its own, since it needs to be orchestrated with our Flask container. Instead, we will combine those two containers into a single system so they can run simultaneously.

This brings us to the last feature that we will see in this section: Docker Compose.

8.1.7 Defining multi-container Docker apps using Docker Compose

Docker Compose is a tool for running multiple containers as a single service.

You might be wondering why we need to have multiple containers? Can't we run everything in a single container? For example, wouldn't it be nice to have both Nginx and uWSGI inside the same container?

The answer is simply no. The reason is that we would lose the ability to have many uWSGI instances but only one Nginx instance. Plus, the container would become enormous. This is where Docker Compose comes into play.

From the developer's perspective, Docker Compose is nothing more than a configuration file in which we define all the containers and how they interact with each other. Again, the cool thing is that we can transfer our entire service to another machine by simply moving the Dockerfiles and the Docker Compose file.

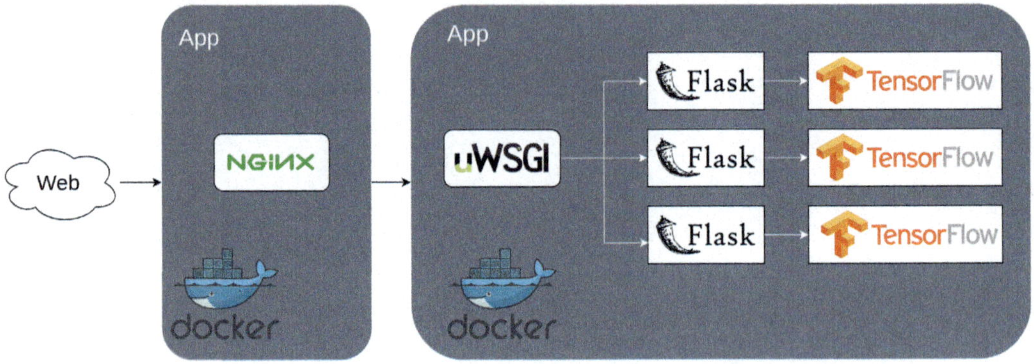

Figure 8.4: A Deep Learning app with Docker compose

Before we begin, we need to install Docker Compose. As previously, it's best to follow the instructions in the original docs.

To define the configuration, we create a `docker-compose.yml` file that declares our two containers and the network interactions.

```
version : "3.7"

services:
    app:
        build: ./app
            container_name: deep-learning-production
        restart: always
        expose:
            - 660

    nginx:
        build: ./nginx
            container_name: nginx
        restart: always
        ports:
            - "80:80"
```

The first thing we need to include is the Docker Compose version and the main services. Here we have an app service with the Tensorflow model and the uWSGI server, and the Nginx service.

Each service has a `build` paramcter that specifies the relative folder path that the service lives in. Docker will look it up when building the image. Moreover, each service has a custom container name. This will be used from other services to define interactions with it. For example, the Nginx config has the following line:

```
uwsgi_pass  app:660
```

As you can see, it matches the name of the uWSGI service declared in the yaml file.

Additionally, we need to restart the service each time the container exits due to failure, to make sure that the services are always up. Finally, we need to define our ports, which honestly is the important part.

Specifically, the uWSGI service should open the 660 port in order to listen for requests from the Nginx server. If you remember, we defined the exact same socket inside our `app.ini` file. Note that the port will be opened inside Docker and will not be exposed in the outer world.

The Nginx service has to open the 80 port in the outer world and map all requests coming there to the 80 port of the container. The first 80 port is chosen randomly but the second 80 port is the listening port that we declared in the Nginx config.

```
server {
    listen 80;
        ...
}
```

So, the flow here goes as follows:

1. Requests from the outer world are coming to the 80 port of our environment
2. They get mapped to the Nginx container's 80 port
3. They get routed to the uWSGI 660 port
4. UWSGI calls the Flask endpoint and executes the Tensorflow inference.
5. UWSGI sends back the response throughout the same pipeline.

See the Figure 8.5 to make sure that you get that right. We can finally build the Docker network with both services using:

```
$ docker-compose build
```

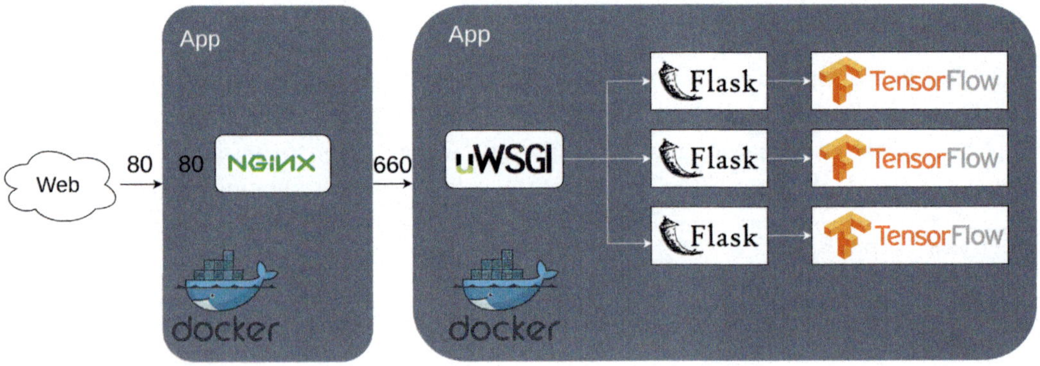

Figure 8.5: Visualization of the ports in a Deep Learning application

and start the docker containers with:

```
$ docker-compose up
```

Let's try to hit our network using our client and ensure that we are using the correct ports.

We run the client script and wait...

```
python client.py
```

If everything worked perfectly, you should be able to see the segmentation mask of a Yorkshire terrier.

So, what is the next step? Obviously, we want to make the application visible to the world. To that end, we will have to deploy it in the cloud and expose it to the web.

8.2 Deploying in a production environment

Once we set up our Docker container and verify that everything works as expected in a local or a test environment, it's time to deploy it in a production environment. Since we are dealing with a web service application, the natural choice is to use a cloud instance. In particular, we will once again use Google Cloud.

This process is 90% similar to what we described when we trained the model on the cloud using a VM instance. So, feel free to revisit the Section 6.2 for a step-by-step guide.

In this section, we will only focus on the three major differences that are present in this particular scenario.

1. How to use Docker in a cloud instance
2. How to expose the instance to the web
3. How to deploy containers in a cloud instance

An important reminder:

In order to serve a model using Docker and Google Cloud, we need to somehow store the trained model in the cloud. This can be done in two ways.

1. Option A: bake the model inside the docker image.
2. Option B: utilize a cloud storage bucket.

In the latter case, we obviously need some functionality to load the model from the bucket at runtime. Option A is not a general practice and it is only recommended for small models.

8.2.1 Using containers in Google Cloud

In order to facilitate containers and Docker inside a VM instance, we basically have 3 options:

1) Create a vanilla VM instance and then install Docker

The workflow of this option is similar to the process of installing Docker in a local environment. All we have to do is to create a VM instance, connect to the instance with ssh and execute all the installation commands for Docker. While this option is quite simple, I wouldn't recommend it. The reason is that the instance won't be optimized for container use, which will result in worse performance or higher cost.

2) Use a Container-Optimized OS image

Container-Optimized Operating System (OS) is a new operating system developed by Google on top of Chromium OS and has one single purpose. To optimize the VM instance for Docker execution in terms of efficiency, security, updates, and low overhead. A big plus is the fact that it requires minimal setup.

To create a Container-Optimized OS instance, the process is quite straightforward. When creating a new instance, we can select the container box. This will open up a few new settings. The container image field expects a Docker image that has been pushed to Container Registry.

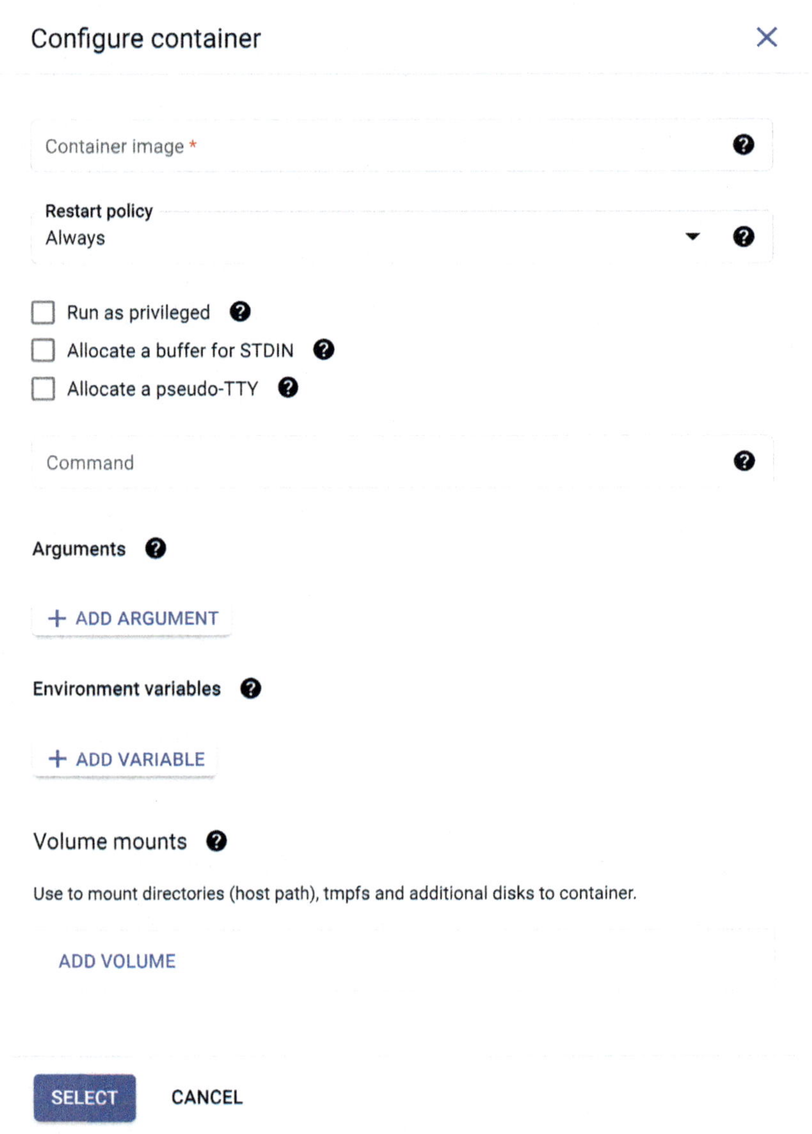

Figure 8.6: Create a container-optimized instance on Google cloud

The Container registry is a single place in the GCP to manage all your Docker images.

So, all we need to do is build and test the image locally and then push it to the registry using the Cloud SDK.

```
$ docker push gcr.io/PROJECT_ID/IMAGE:TAG
```

And that's all we need to do.

3) Use a public VM image

Google Cloud comes with a variety of predefined and highly optimized images for all sorts of use cases. These images can be used as a "template" when we are creating a VM instance. And of course, there are a lot of them that have Docker pre-installed.

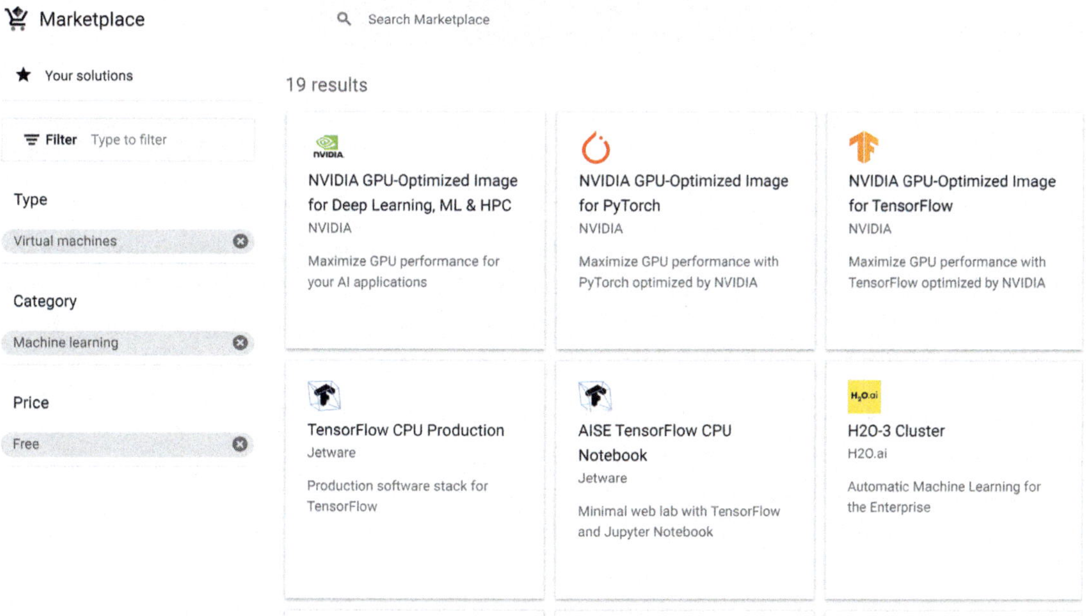

Figure 8.7: List of public VM images on Google cloud

8.2.2 Allowing network traffic to the instance

The second major problem that we need to solve is how to allow HTTP traffic to the instance so that users can send requests for inference. Once again, this can be configured in the creation stage by checking the correct checkboxes.

By doing that , as shown in the Figure 8.8, we assign an external IP to the instance, which can be used to send requests. Assuming that the Docker environment has been configured properly and the correct ports have been exposed, our application will be

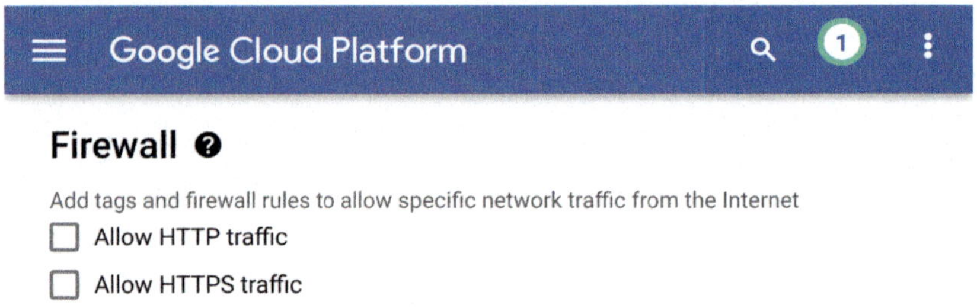

Figure 8.8: HTTP options during VM creation

deployed correctly. Moreover, we can modify networking settings as we wish by setting up firewall rules (e.g. allowing or banning specific traffic).

8.2.3 Deploying in Google Cloud

So far so good. We created our Docker-powered instances, we allowed external requests to them. But how do we actually deploy our container in them? The answer depends on what type of image we used during the creation process. That's why we will examine each one separately. In all cases, though, we have to make sure that our Docker image has been pushed in the Container Registry. So regardless the type of image, we will need to build and push the Docker image.

```
$ docker build -t deep-learning-production:1.0 .
$ docker tag deep-learning-production:1.0
    gcr.io/PROJECT_ID/deep-learning-production:1.0
$ docker push gcr.io/PROJECT_ID/deep-learning-production:1.0
```

Let's now see how we can deploy the pushed container on each case. For simplicity reasons, I assume that we only deploy our application container without Nginx and Docker Compose. The process with Docker Compose is quite similar but a tad more complicated, so I will leave that for you.

1) Create a vanilla VM instance and then install Docker

In the case that we created a standard instance and installed Docker manually, all we have to do is connect into the instance and simply run the Docker container located in Container Registry.

```
$ docker run --publish 80:8080  --name dlp
    gcr.io/PROJECT_ID/deep-learning-production:1.0
```

2) Use a Container-Optimized OS image

If we initialized a Container-Optimized OS image, then we have nothing else to do. During the creation process, we assigned a Docker container in the image. This instructs GCP to spin up Docker and run the corresponding container as soon as the instance is functional. So, everything is taken care of for us behind the scenes.

But what if we want to update our Docker container and redeploy the app? This is straightforward and can be done with a simple command. Assuming that we have built and pushed the new image, we can run:

```
$ gcloud compute instances update-container VM_INSTANCE_NAME \
  --container-image gcr.io/PROJECT_ID/deep-learning-production:2.0
```

3) Use a public VM image

Having set up an instance with a public VM image doesn't affect deployment at all. The process is identical with the one we used in the first case. Once again, we need to connect to the instance and run the appropriate Docker container.

8.3 Continuous Integration and Delivery (CI / CD)

Continuous Integration (CI) and Continuous Delivering (CD) is a set of practices and pipelines that automates the building, testing, and deployment process. Famous frameworks include Jenkins and CircleCI. GCP has its own CI/CD service, called Cloud Build.

But why do we need CI/CD? CI/CD workflows allow the engineering team to update the application in a structural manner. Each workflow consists of a sequence of predefined steps that are processed in order. These steps can include things such as:

- Unit and Acceptance tests
- Compilation
- Container building and pushing
- Dependencies installation
- Deployment

Each workflow can be triggered by a distinct event. Most commonly, a workflow is triggered after new code is being merged into the main branch of our repository. After triggering, a new job is created. The job is responsible for executing all the steps in a sequential order. If all steps are processed correctly, the workflow finishes, and the new version of our application is deployed. If, however, there was some error in one of the steps, the job is usually responsible for "undoing" everything and reverting back to the original state.

To showcase the effectiveness of CI/CD workflows, we will use Cloud Build to automate our deployment pipeline. The workflow will be triggered once a new commit is pushed in the main branch. After the trigger, the workflow will:

1. Build the new Docker image
2. Push the image into Container Registry
3. Deploy the new container to the VM instance

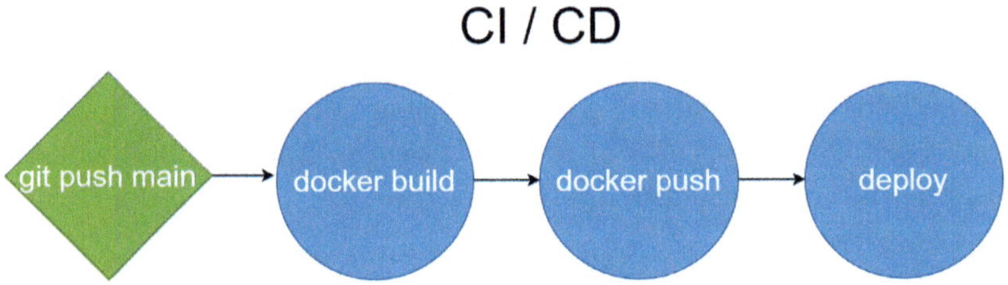

Figure 8.9: Continuous Integration and Continuous Delivery

To create a new workflow, we first need to create a trigger event. This can be done programmatically or from the cloud console.

```
gcloud beta builds triggers create github \
    --repo-name=MY_REPO_NAME \
    --repo-owner=MY_REPO_OWNER \
    --branch-pattern=main \
    --build-config=cloudbuild.yaml \
    --service-account=SERVICE_ACCOUNT \
    --require-approval
```

This trigger will associate Cloud Build with our Github repository and it will trigger a build when a new commit is pushed on the specified branch.

Afterwards, we need to construct a `cloudbuild.yaml` file inside our project. The `cloudbuild.yaml` will define the necessary steps and their order. A sample file would look like this:

```
steps:
- name: 'gcr.io/cloud-builders/docker'
```

```
  args: ['build', '-t',
    'gcr.io/$PROJECT_ID/deep-learning-production:latest']
  id: 'build-image'
  waitFor: ['-']
- name: 'gcr.io/cloud-builders/docker'
  args: ['push',
    'gcr.io/$PROJECT_ID/deep-learning-production:latest']
  id: 'push-image-to-container-registry'
  waitFor: ['build-image']
- name: 'gcr.io/cloud-builders/gcloud'
  args:
  - 'compute'
  - 'instances'
  - 'update-container'
  - 'MY_INSTANCE_NAME'
  - ' --container-image'
  - 'gcr.io/$PROJECT_ID/deep-learning-production:latest'
  waitFor: ['push-image-to-container-registry']
  id: 'deploy-to-vm-instance'
```

As you can see, we have a set of steps. Each step has a unique id, a command and a `waitFor` argument. The command consists of the `name` and the `args`. The `name` indicates the program/service that will be executed, and the `args` are the arguments of the execution. The first step runs a `docker build`, the second a `docker push` and the third a `gcloud compute instance update-container`. Finally, the `waitFor` forces each step to wait for the previous one to be finished.

Chapter 9

Scaling

In this chapter:

- How to scale your application
- How to use Kubernetes with deep learning
- Why Kubernetes is a good choice for ML systems

Scalability is undoubtedly a high-level problem that we will all be thrilled to have. Reaching a point where we need to incorporate more machines and resources to handle the traffic, is a dream come true for many start-ups.

However, many teams and engineers don't pay the necessary attention to it. To tackle scaling issues, one needs to have a clear plan from the beginning. But in practice, we first need to focus on squeezing our model's performance, and deal with scaling later.

9.1 A journey from 1 to millions of users

In this section, **we will follow along with a small AI start-up on its journey to scale from 1 user to millions of them**. We will discuss what's a typical process to handle a steady growth of the user base, and what tools and techniques one can incorporate. We will examine ML characteristics that differ from normal software applications. To be able to grasp the whole picture, we will follow a spherical and theoretical approach. That means we will not dig into code.

Let's rewind. Remember that we built a standard web application around our model and deployed it. Assume for a moment that the application has not been deployed yet and that we want to compare our options based on how easy it will be to scale the infrastructure in the future. So, what is our next step here?

At this point we basically have two options:

1. set up our own server, host it there and worry about all the scalability as we grow.
2. deploy the application in a cloud provider and take advantage of the ready and already-optimized infrastructure.

I will assume that you want to go with the second option so let's stick with Google Cloud. This way, we have tangible examples to illustrate as a showcase. For those who are unfamiliar with Google Cloud Services (GCS), here is a glossary section outlining the used components.

Glossary

- **Compute engine**: enables users to launch and manage virtual machines on demand.
- **Virtual private cloud**: network functionality among GC resources.
- **Load balancing**: globally distributed load balancer.
- **Cloud memorystore**: a managed in-memory service based on cache systems such as Redis and Memcached.
- **Cloud tasks**: distributed task queues for asynchronous execution.
- **Cloud DNS**: DNS serving from Google's worldwide network.
- **Cloud Build**: CI/CD platform.
- **Cloud source repositories**: private git repositories.
- **Pub/Sub**: asynchronous messaging system.
- **Cloud functions**: serverless execution environment.
- **Cloud storage**: object storage system.
- **Monitoring**: systems that provide visibility into the performance, uptime, and overall health of applications.

- **Cloud logging**: real-time log management and analysis.
- **Error reporting**: counts and aggregates crashes from services based on their stack traces.

Now we are ready. Shall we begin?

9.1.1 First iterations of the machine learning app

First iteration

Once we're done experimenting with our model accuracy, we want to deploy and expose it to the web.

The first step would be to create a VM instance on Google Cloud's compute engine. We copy the whole project, the trained model weights, we allow HTTP traffic, and connect our domain name to it.

The model is up and running, and is visible to users through our domain. People are starting to send requests, everything works as expected, the system remains highly responsive, the model's accuracy seems to be on good levels, and we are incredibly happy about it.

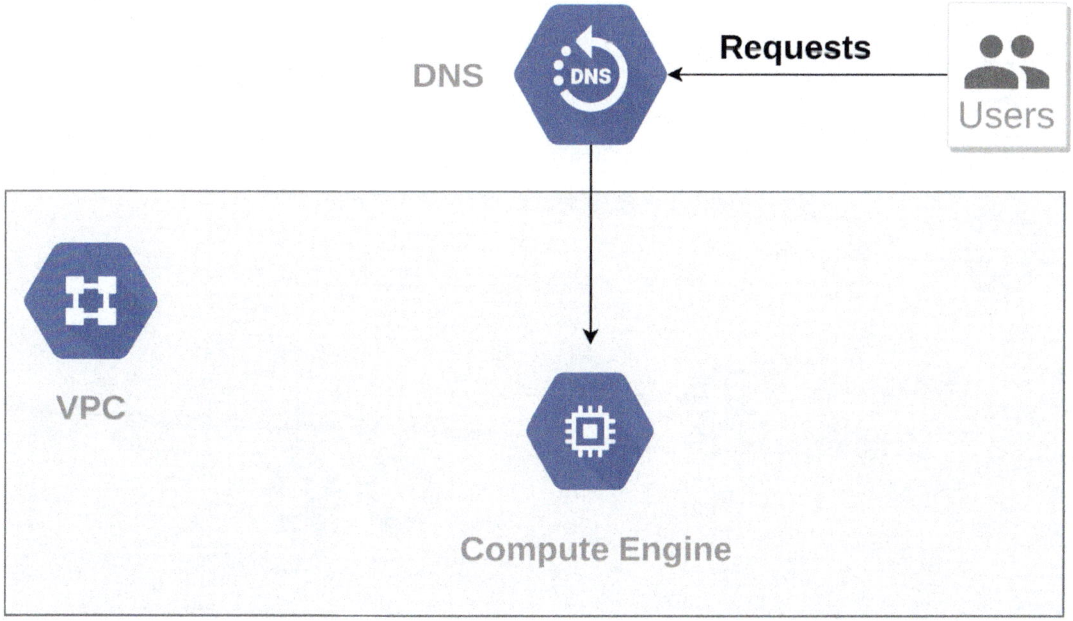

Figure 9.1: A vanilla Deep Learning app on cloud

Issues with this approach

So, we have a monolithic app, hosted in one virtual machine, which requires a bit of manual work to deploy new changes and restart the service, but it's not bad. After doing that for a few weeks, some problems are starting to arise.

- Deployments require too much manual work
- Dependencies are starting to get out of sync as we add new library versions and new models.
- Debugging is not straightforward.

Second iteration: logs and CI/CD pipeline

To solve some of those problems, we add a new **CI/CD pipeline** and we manage to automate tasks such as building, testing and deployment.

We also add some **logs** so we can access the instance and discover what's wrong. Perhaps we can even migrate from a basic Virtual Machine (VM) to a **deep learning specific VM** (provided by GCP) which is highly optimized for deep learning applications. It comes with Tensorflow, CUDA and other necessary stuff pre-installed, helping us alleviate some of the manual work.

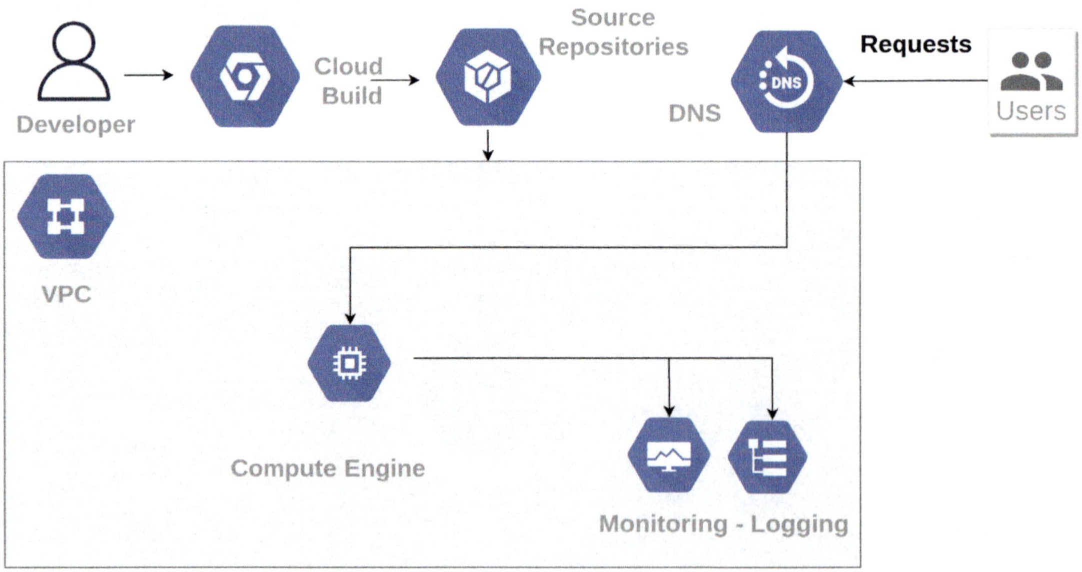

Figure 9.2: Continuous integration, deployment and monitoring

Third iteration: Docker container

But deployment and dependencies are still an issue. To address that, we **wrap the application inside a Docker container**, put it in the VM and we're good to go. Again, we can use a ready-to-use deep learning-specific container. As a result, every time we need to add a new library version or a new model, we change the Dockerfile, rebuild the container and redeploy. And things are looking good once more.

After a while though, the app is starting to become popular, more and more users are joining. Hence, the VM instance is starting to struggle, response times go up, hardware utilization is at a high level. I'm afraid that we have to scale.

9.1.2 Vertical vs horizontal scaling

Fourth iteration: scaling up

Vertical scaling (scaling-up) is when we **add more power (CPU, Memory, GPU)** to an existing machine to handle the traffic.

Our first reaction is to scale vertically as shown in the Figure 9.3. So, we create a new bigger instance with more memory, better CPU and better GPU's. After a while, the instance is starting to struggle again. We then create an even bigger one. After doing that a couple of times, we're starting to hit a limit and realize that we can't keep scaling up.

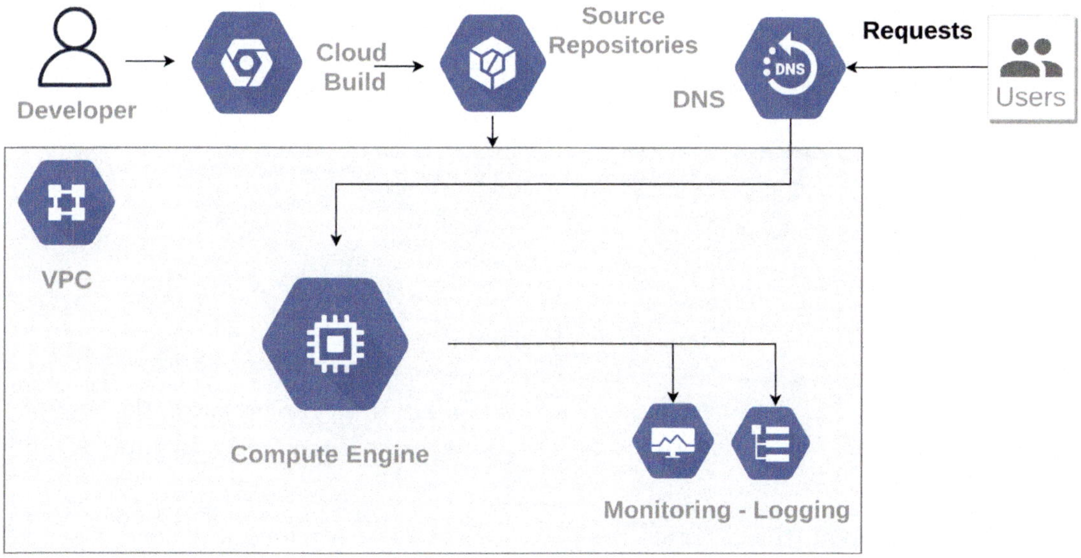

Figure 9.3: Vertical scaling

Consequently, we have to scale out.

Fifth iteration: scaling out

Horizontal scaling (scaling out) is when we **add more machines** to the network and share the processing and memory workload across them. This simply means: create a new VM instance. We will then replicate the application and have them both run and serve traffic simultaneously. Note that this usually requires no changes to the existing code.

But how do we decide which instance gets recieves the requests? How do we keep the traffic even between them? This is where load balancers come into the game.

A load balancer is a device that distributes network traffic across multiple machines and ensures that no single server bears too much load, by spreading the traffic. Therefore, it increases the capacity, reliability and availability of the system.

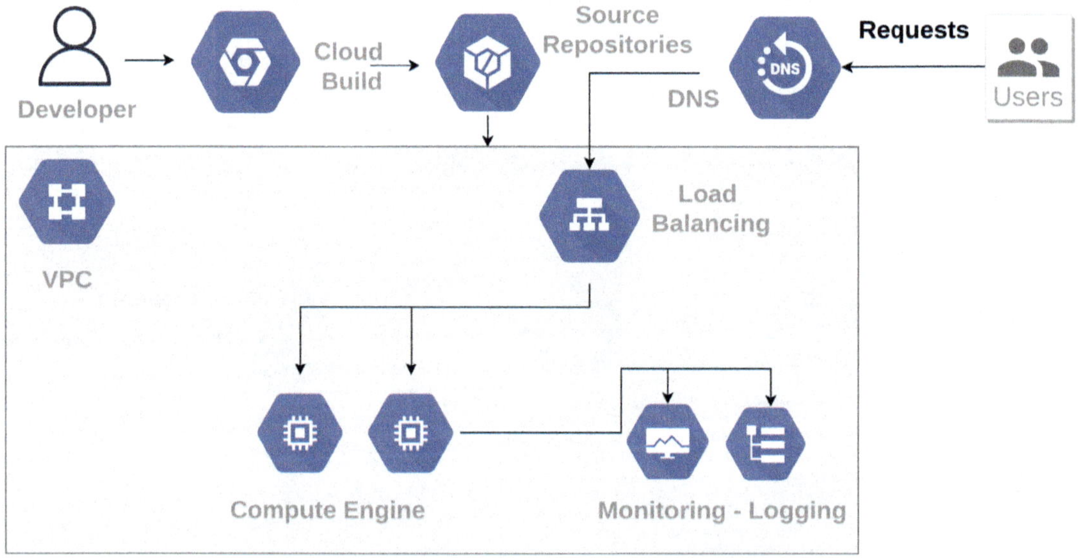

Figure 9.4: Horizontal scaling

After including a second instance and a load balancer in our system, the traffic is handled perfectly. Neither instance is struggling, and their response time is going back down.

The great thing about this architecture is that it can take us a long way down the road. Honestly it is what most of us will probably ever need. **As the traffic grows, we can keep adding more and more instances and load balance the traffic between**

them. We can also have instances in different geographic regions (or availability zones as Amazon Web Services/AWS calls them). This enables us to minimize the response time in all parts of the world.

Interesting fact: we don't have to worry about the load balancer when it comes to different geographic regions. Why? Because most cloud providers such as GCP offer load balancers that scale requests among multiple regions.

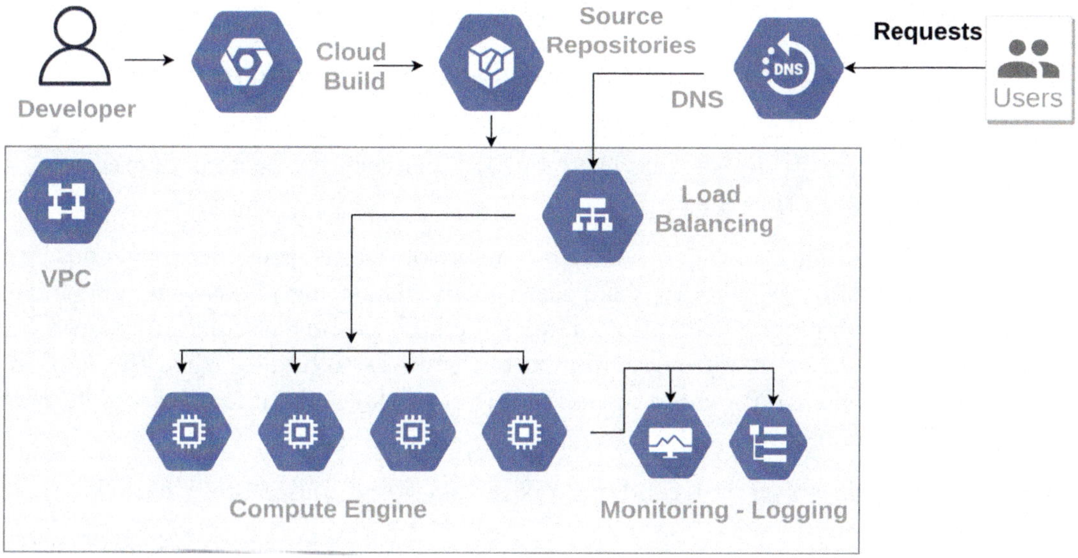

Figure 9.5: Horizontal scaling on a higher degree

Load balancers also provide robust security. They entail encryption/decryption, user authentication and health checks to ensure that all connections are healthy. They also have capabilities for monitoring and debugging.

Let's do a quick recap: so far, we managed to ensure availability and reliability using load balancers and multiple instances. In parallel, we alleviated the pain of deployments with containers and CI/CD, and we have a basic form of logging and monitoring. I'd state that we are in pretty good shape.

As I said before, in the vast majority of use cases, this approach is 100% enough. But there are times when unexpected things occur.

A very common example is **sudden spikes in traffic**. Sometimes we see a very big increase in the number of incoming requests. And trust me: it is more common that you may want to believe. What's the course of action here?

Someone might think that we can increase the capacity of our machines to a level that it can handle the spikes on the request rate. But that would be a huge amount of unused resources and, most importantly, of money not well spent. One solution to this problem is autoscaling.

9.1.3 Autoscaling

Autoscaling is a method used in cloud computing that **alters the amount of computational resources based on the load**. Typically, this means that the number of instances goes up or down automatically, based on a variety of metrics.

Autoscaling comes in 2 main forms: **scheduled scaling and dynamic scaling**.

- In scheduled scaling, we know in advance that the traffic will vary in a specific period of time. To tackle this, we manually instruct the system to create more instances during this time.
- Dynamic scaling, on the other hand, monitors some predefined metrics and scales the instances when they surpass a limit. These metrics can include things like CPU or memory utilization, requests count, response time and more. For example, we can configure our number of instances to double when the requests rate is more than 100 per second. When the rate falls, the instances will go back to their normal state.

And that efficiently solves the random spikes issue. One more box checked for our application.

9.1.4 Cache mechanisms

Another great way to minimize the response time of our application is to use some sort of cache mechanism . Sometimes we may see many identical requests coming in (although this rarely will be the case for computer vision apps). If that's the case, we can **avoid hitting our servers many times and we can simply cache the response of the first request and send it to all the other users**.

A cache is nothing more than a storage system that saves responses so that future requests can be served faster, as depicted in the Figure 9.6.

An important thing to know here is that we have to calibrate our caching mechanism efficiently, so that we avoid either caching too much data which we won't use often, or keeping the cache idle for a very long time.

9.1.5 Monitoring alerts

One of the most important and, honestly, most annoying parts of an application that's been served to many users, are alerts. Sometimes things crash. Maybe there was a

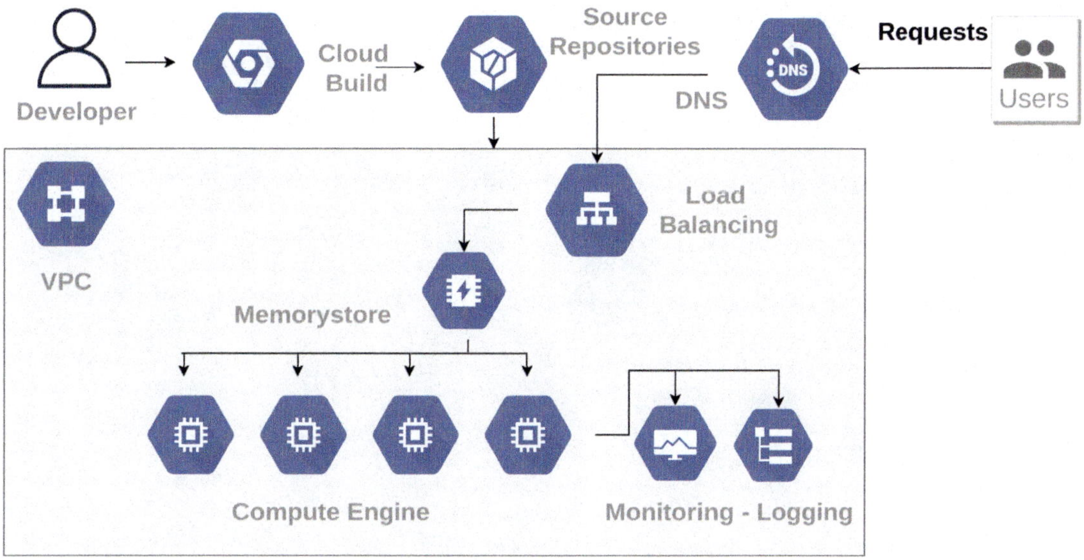

Figure 9.6: Addition of a caching mechanism

bug in the code, or the autoscaling system didn't work, or a network failure occurred, or there was a power outage. There are literally hundreds of things that can go wrong. If our application has only a few users, this might not be that critical. But if we serve millions of them, every minute our app is down, we're losing money.

That's why we must have an **alerting system** in place, so we can jump in as quickly as possible and fix the error. Being on-call is an integral part of being a software engineer. This applies to machine learning engineers as well. Although sometimes in real-life projects that's not the case. But machine learning models can have bugs and be affected by all the aforementioned things.

No need to build a custom solution. Most cloud providers provide monitoring systems that 1) track various predefined metrics 2) enable visualizations and dashboards for us to check their progress over time and 3) notify us when an incident happens.

A monitoring system combined with logging and an error reporting module, is all we need in order to sleep well at night. So, I highly recommend including it in your machine learning application.

Up until this point, most of the concepts mentioned apply to all kinds of software. That's why from now on we will see some examples that are needed only for machine learning applications. Although the tools that we will use are not AI-specific, the concepts and the problems behind them are unique to the field.

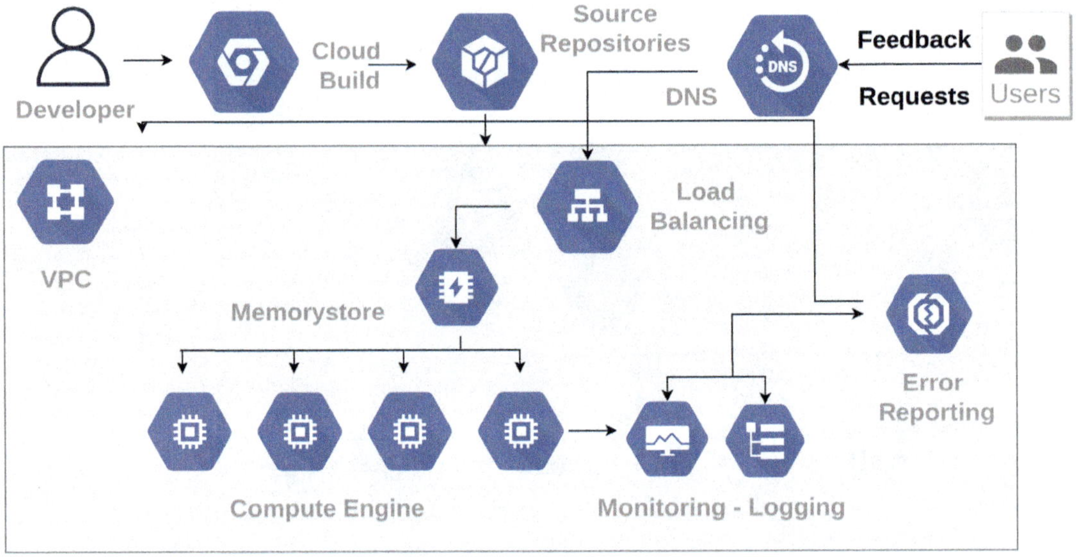

Figure 9.7: Addition of error reporting and alerting system

9.1.6 Retraining machine learning models

As the model serves more and more users, the data distribution is starting to shift. As a result, the **model's accuracy gradually deteriorates**. This is simply inevitable, and it happens to most ML applications. Thus, we need to **build a retraining loop to train the model with new data and redeploy it as a new version**. We could find the data from an external source but sometimes this isn't possible. That's why we should be able to use internal data.

With our current architecture this is not possible as we don't store any predictions or user feedbacks regarding the predictions. First of all, we need to find a way to **get feedback from our users and use it as labels in our retraining**. This means that we will need an endpoint where clients can use to send their explicit feedback related to a specific prediction. Alternatively, we can derive a form of implicit feedback from other sources.

If we assume that we have that in place, the next step is to **store that data**. We need a database. Here, we have many solutions, and it is a very common debate between teams. Most scalability experts will claim that we should start with a SQL database and move to a NoSQL when the audience reaches a specific point. Although this is true in 90% of the cases, someone could argue that ML is not one of them. ML data are usually unstructured, and they can't be organized in tabular format.

From a scalability perspective both SQL and NoSQL can handle a pretty big amount of

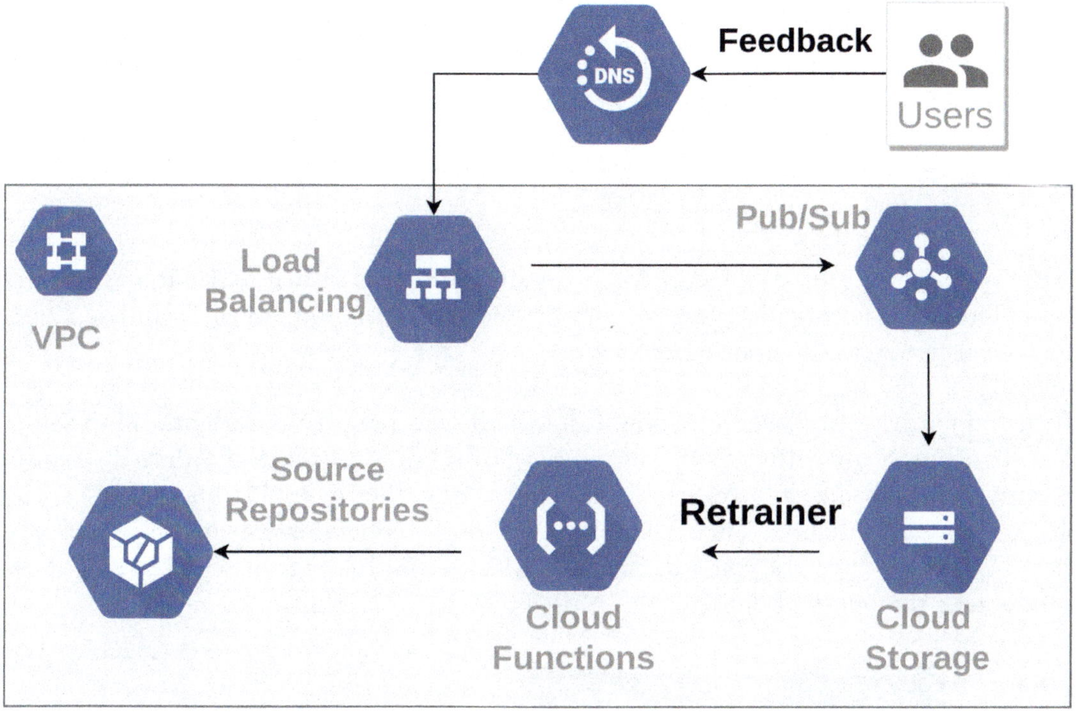

Figure 9.8: Retraining Deep Learning models loop

data with NoSQL having a slight advantage in the area. I'm not going to go into many details here about how scalability works on databases, but I will mention some basic concepts for those who want to look into them. For SQL folks, we have techniques such as master-slave replication, sharding, denormalization, federation while for NoSQL the scalability patterns are custom to the specific database (key-value, document, column based, graph).

And, of course, we can use a object storage solution if possible. The crucial thing is that we have the data stored. As a result, we can **build training jobs by feeding those data into the model**, save the new model (weights), and redeploy the new model into production. And we can repeat this process according to our needs.

Two notes here:

- The model versioning problem is already solved by containers because we can create a new image for the new model and deploy.
- The storage of the model weights is also solved either by using a database or more preferably with an object storage service (such as Google Cloud Storage)

which is extremely scalable and efficient.

However, the problem of running multiple, high-intensive, simultaneous training jobs remains. Again, we have several different solutions.

1. We can spin up new instances/containers on demand, run the jobs, and remove them after completion.

2. We can use a distributed data processing framework such as Hadoop or Spark. These frameworks are able to handle enormous amounts of data and scale efficiently across different machines.

Such frameworks are based on some form of the map-reduce paradigm. Map-reduce is a distributed algorithm that works as follows: we first split the data in groups, execute a processing step on each one (map), and then combine the results into a single dataset (reduce). This is similar to the all-reduce algorithm we explored in distributed training. As you can imagine, this method is highly scalable and it can handle huge amounts of data.

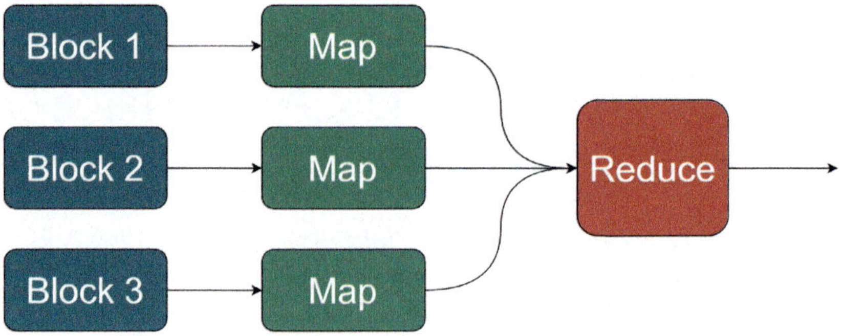

Figure 9.9: Map-reduce example

9.1.7 Model A/B testing

Another need that might appear, especially after having retraining in place, is A/B testing. **A/B testing refers to the process of trying out different models in production by sending different loads of traffic into each one of them**. Again, containers solve this issue out of the box because we can deploy different versions of them at the same time. To distribute the traffic, we can configure the load balancer to send a constant amount of traffic to each one. For example, we can send only 5% of the traffic into the new model and keep the other 95% for the old one.

9.1.8 Offline inference

Last but not least, one can execute offline inferences . Predicting in real-time is not always feasible or desired. There are plenty of use cases where the model simply can't infer in a couple of seconds or our application does not need a real-time response. One good example is video processing which often requires huge inference times. In such cases, the alternative is to have an **offline inference pipeline and perform inference in an asynchronous manner**.

Asynchronous means that the user won't have to wait for the model to generate the prediction. They will be notified later about the completion (or not nodified at all). But how do we build such pipelines?

The most common approach is **message queues**.

In general, a message queue is a form of asynchronous service to service communication. A queue stores messages coming from a producer and ensures that all of them will be processed only once by a single consumer. A message queue can have multiple consumers and producers.

Figure 9.10: A message queue

In our case, a producer will be an instance that receives an inference request and sends the request to a worker. The workers will execute the inference based on the sent features. Instead of sending the messages directly to the worker (aka the consumer), it will send it to a message queue. The message queue receives messages from different producers and sends them to the different consumers. But why do we need a queue?

A few characteristics that make message queues ideal are:

- They ensure that the message will always be consumed.
- They can be scaled almost effortlessly by adding more consumer/producer instances.
- They operate asynchronously meaning that they decouple the consumer from the producer.
- They try to maintain the order of messages.
- They provide the ability to prioritize messages.

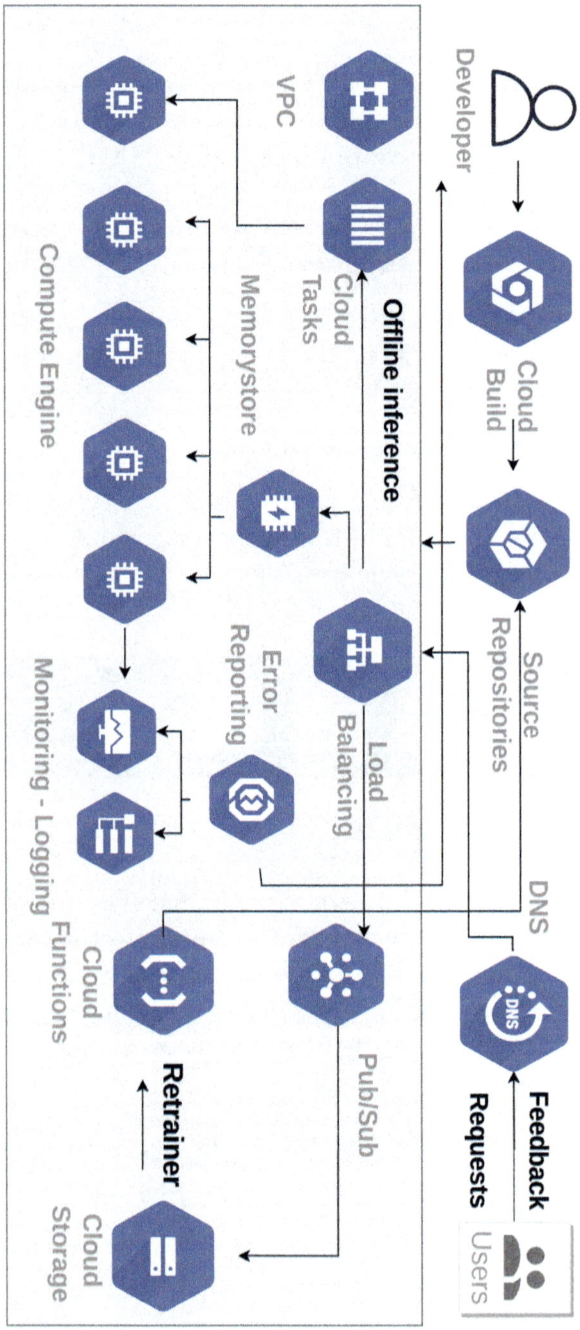

Figure 9.11: A fully functional Deep Learning app

An offline inference pipeline can either be executed in **batches or one-by-one**. In both cases, we can use message queues. In Google Cloud, we can use the Cloud Tasks service that allows us to manage distributed message queues.

Please note that, in the case of batching, we should have a system that combines many inferences together and sends them back to the correct user, as we discussed in Chapter 5. Batching can happen either on the instance level or on the service level.

And that officially ends our scalability journey. The entire infrastructure can be found in the Figure 9.11. From now on, all we can do is fine-tune the application in the best possible way. Solutions include:

- Splitting functionality into different services by building a microservices architecture.
- Analysing in depth the entire stack and optimizing wherever it's possible.
- As a last resort, we can start building custom solutions.

In this section, I tried to give an overview of how companies' infrastructure evolves over the years as they grow and acquire more users. Scaling an application is by no means easy. ML systems make things tougher since they introduce a whole new set of issues and constraints.

The reason why I provided a general overview before we proceed on specific scaling tools and methods, is that now we all have a clear idea of what lies ahead in real-life projects. In the next section, we will discuss how to use the aforementioned techniques in practice, utilizing Google's cloud platform and Kubernetes.

9.2 Growing with Kubernetes

A very good approach, in my honest opinion, for deploying and scaling a deep learning application is to use Kubernetes and Google Cloud. The question is why? We should not pick frameworks just because they're trendy and everyone else seems to use them. In this section we will explore what Kubernetes is, why it might be the best option to deploy ML applications, and what features it provides to help us maintain and scale our infrastructure. As far as Google Cloud concerns, it is an obvious choice because Kubernetes is partially built by a Google team and Google Kubernetes Engine (GKE) is highly coupled with it.

9.2.1 What is Kubernetes?

In Chapter 8, we discussed what containers are, and what advantages they provide over classic methods such as Virtual Machines. To recap, containers give us isolation, portability, easy experimentation, and consistency over different environments. Plus, they are far more lightweight than VMs. If you are convinced about using containers and Docker, Kubernetes will come as a natural choice.

Kubernetes is a container orchestration system that automates deployment, scaling and management of containerized applications.

In other words, it helps us handle multiple containers with the same or different applications using declarative configurations. Because of my Greek origin, I couldn't stop myself from telling you that Kubernetes means helmsman or captain in Greek. It is the person/system that controls the whole ship and makes sure that everything is working as expected.

Some reasons to use Kubernetes:

1. It manages the entire container's lifecycle from creation to deletion.
2. It provides a high level of abstraction with configuration files.
3. It maximizes hardware utilization.
4. It's an infrastructure-as-Code (IaC) framework, which means that everything is an API call whether it's scaling containers or provisioning a load balancer.

Despite the high-level abstractions it provides, it also comes with some very important features that we use in our every-day ML DevOps life:

- Scheduling: It decides where and when containers should run.
- Lifecycle and health: It ensures that all containers are up all the time and it spins up new ones when an old container die.
- Scaling: It provides an easy way to scale containers up or down manually or automatically (autoscaling).
- Load balancing.
- Logging and monitoring systems.

Honestly, the trickiest part about Kubernetes is its naming of different components. Once you get the grasp of it, everything will just click in your mind. In fact, it's not that different from standard software systems.

9.2.2 Getting started with Kubernetes

In modern web applications, we usually have a server that is exposed to the web and is receiving requests from different clients. Traditionally the server is either a physical machine or a VM instance. When we have increased traffic, we add another instance in the server and manage the load using a load balancer. But we might also have many servers hosting different applications in the same system. Then, we need an external load balancer to route the requests to the different internal load balancer, which will finally send it to the correct instance, as illustrated in the Figure 9.12.

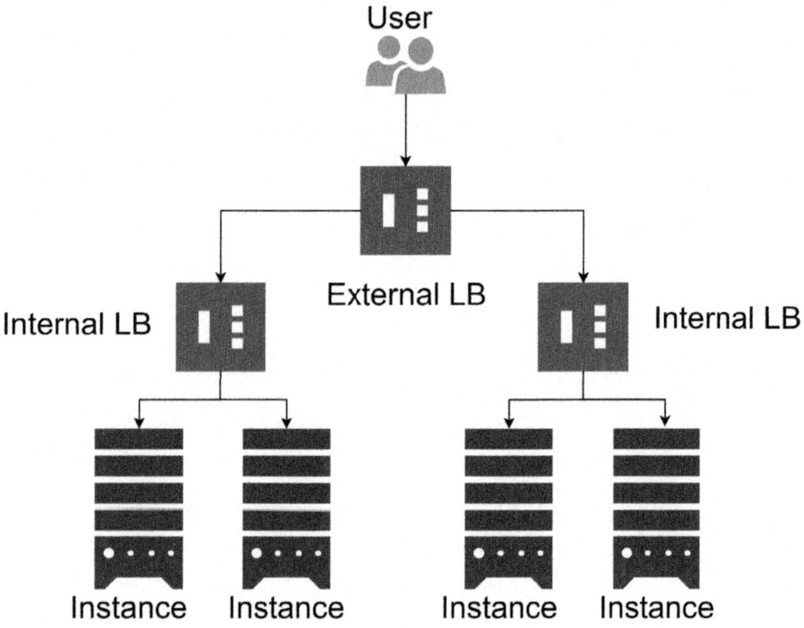

Figure 9.12: A typical web application

Kubernetes does the exact same thing but calls everything by different names. The internal load balancer is called a Service and the external load balancer is called Ingress. And instead of calling the application containers as containers, it calls them Pods.

A **node** is a physical or virtual machine that runs many pods (aka containers), and a **cluster** is simply a collection of nodes. And to make things more confusing, we can either have a physical cluster or a virtual cluster that includes multiple clusters (this is called **namespace**).

I know there are too many new terms, but things are quite simple actually if you keep in mind the mapping of the different definitions.

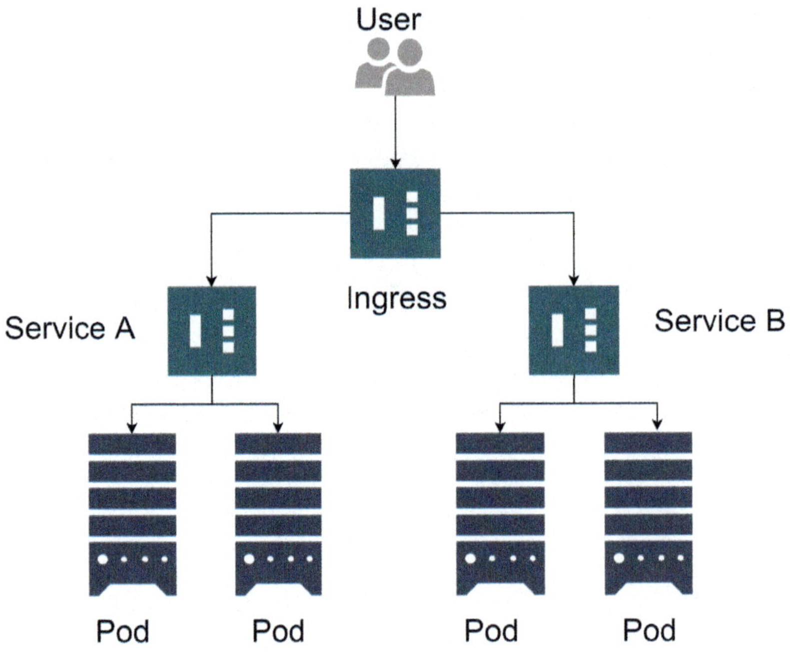

Figure 9.13: A typical web application with Kubernetes

Without Kubernetes	With Kubernetes
Containers	Pod
Internal Load Balancer	Service
External Load Balancer	Ingress
Application	Deployment
Physical Machine	Node
Cluster of Machines	Cluster
Virtual Cluster	Namespace

Let's see how things work in practice to hopefully make more sense of it. To do that, we will deploy our containerized application in Google Cloud using Google Kubernetes Engine (GKE).

Before we proceed, let's clarify a few things. In Chapter 7 and 8, we saw how to utilize Nginx, Docker and Docker Compose to handle the serving and the load balancing. As we will extensively see, Kubernetes and GKE take care of all that by themselves. That's why in this section, we will disregard some of the work we did in those chapters. In fact, we will keep only the Docker image containing our Flask/uWSGI application with the endpoint for serving predictions. This will be referred as `deep-learning-in-production` in the following code snippets.

This means that we will no longer utilize Nginx and Docker Compose. Kubernetes can be thought as an alternative to Nginx and Docker Compose. Please note that most of the problems solved below, can also be addressed by using the existing techniques. This of course doesn't mean that one should always choose one or the other for their projects. It entirely depends on the application needs. For example, small applications with low traffic might be better served with Nginx, while large-scale projects might benefit from the flexibility of Kubernetes. The choice is up to the infrastructure team.

9.2.3 Deploying with Google Kubernetes Engine

Google Kubernetes Engine (GKE) is a Google Cloud service that provides an environment and APIs to manage Kubernetes applications deployed in Google's infrastructure. Conceptually, it is similar to what Compute Engine is for VMs. In fact, GKE runs on top of Compute Engine instances, but that's another story.

The first thing we need to take care of is how to interact with Google Cloud and GKE. We have three options here:

1. Use Google Cloud's UI directly (Google Cloud console).
2. Use Google's integrated terminal (cloud shell).
3. Handle everything from our local terminal.

For educational purposes, I will go with the third option. We will explain and implement the deployment using the following steps

1. Install `gcloud` and `kubectl`.
2. Transfer local files and Dockerfile.
3. Set up a Kubernetes deployment.
4. Set up a Kubernetes service.

1) Installing `gcloud` and `kubectl`

To configure our local terminal to interact with Kubernetes and GKE, we need to install two tools: Google Cloud SDK (`gcloud`) and the Kubernetes CLI (`kubect`).

Remember that I told you that in Kubernetes everything is an API call? Well, we can use those two tools to do pretty much everything.

To install `gcloud`, we can follow the very good official documentation. For `kubectl`, the official Kubernetes docs are quite good as well. Both of them shouldn't take that long, as they are only a couple of commands.

GKE can only be managed inside a Google Cloud project so we can either create a new one or use an existing one.

To deploy our application, we first want to create a new cluster by running:

```
$ gcloud container clusters create CLUSTER_NAME --num-nodes=1
```

We can verify that the cluster is created correctly using Google Cloud console. We should see something like the Figure 9.14.

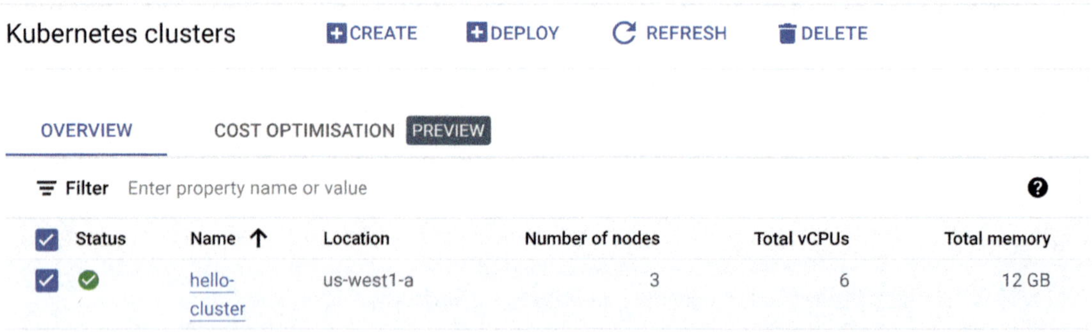

Figure 9.14: Kubernetes engine on Google cloud

Note that I chose to use 3 nodes in this cluster.

The next thing is to configure `kubectl` to work with GKE and the cluster we just created. If we initialized `gcloud`, we should be good to go by running the below command:

```
$ gcloud container clusters get-credentials CLUSTER_NAME
```

After that, every `kubectl` command will be automatically mapped to our GKE cluster. Our cluster and nodes are initialized and waiting for our application to be deployed.

2) Transfering local files and Dockerfile

Kubernetes defines **Deployment** as a specific term that represents an object that manages an application, typically by running pods. So, **to deploy any application we need to create a Deployment**. Each deployment is associated with a Docker image. In GKE's case, the Docker image needs to be placed in the Google Container's Registry so that GKE can pull it and build the container.

To push an image in the container's registry, we can use the following set of commands:

```
$ HOSTNAME = gcr.io
$ PROJECT_ID = deep-learning-production
$ IMAGE = dlp
$ TAG= 0.1
$ SOURCE_IMAGE = deep-learning-in-production
$ docker tag ${IMAGE} $ HOSTNAME /${PROJECT_ID}/${IMAGE}:${TAG}
$ docker push $ HOSTNAME /${PROJECT_ID}/${IMAGE}:${TAG}
```

The above commands will simply transfer the Dockerfile for the local image and all the necessary files to the remote registry. To make sure that it's been pushed, check out the uploaded images using:

```
$ gcloud container images list-tags [HOSTNAME]/[PROJECT_ID]/[IMAGE]
```

Once the image is uploaded, we can build the container by executing:

```
$ gcloud builds submit --tag gcr.io/deep-learning-in-production/app .
```

3) Setting up a Kubernetes Deployment

Following that, we can create a new Kubernetes Deployment. We can either do this with a simple `kubectl` command:

```
$ kubectl create deployment deep-learning-production
    --image=gcr.io/dlp-project/deep-learning-in-production 1.0
```

Or we can create a configuration file (`deployment.yaml`) to be more precise with our options.

```
apiVersion: apps/v1
kind: Deployment
metadata:
    name: deep-learning-production
spec:
    replicas: 3
    selector:
        matchLabels:
            app: dlp
    template:
        metadata:
```

```
            labels:
                app: dlp
        spec:
            containers:
                - name: dlp
                    image: gcr.io/$PROJECT_ID/$IMAGE
                    ports:
                        - containerPort: 8080
                    env:
                        - name: PORT
                        value: "8080"
```

What did we define here? In a few words, the above file tells Kubernetes that it needs to create a Deployment object, named "deep-learning-production", with three distinct pods (**replicas**). The pods will contain our previously built image and will expose the 8080 port to receive external traffic. For more details on how to structure the yaml file, one needs to delve into the official Kubernetes documentation. Remember one size never fits all.

Nonetheless, isn't it awesome that we can do so many things using a simple config file? That would normally take us multiple commands and installations. Now, there is no "ssh" into the instance, no installing a bunch of things, no searching the UI for the correct button. Just a small config file.

By applying the `deployments.yaml` config as shown below, the deployment will automatically be created:

```
$ kubectl apply -f deployment.yaml
```

We can now track our deployment with `kubectl`:

```
$ kubectl get deployments
```

Which will list all available deployments.

```
NAME     READY   UP-TO-DATE  AVAILABLE   AGE
deep-learning-production    1/1 1    1   40s
```

Same for the pods:

```
$ kubectl get pods
```

As we can see, all 3 pods are up and running

```
NAME    READY   STATUS  RESTARTS    AGE
deep-learning-production-57c495f96c-lblrk   1/1 Running 0   40s
deep-learning-production-57c495f96c-sdfui   1/1 Running 0   40s
deep-learning-production-57c495f96c-plgio   1/1 Running 0   40s
```

4) Set up a Kubernetes Service

Due to the fact that we have many pods running, we should have a load balancer in front of them. As I mentioned before, Kubernetes calls internal load balancers as Services. Note that pods are ephemeral and can be restarted without any warning. To that end, **Services provide a single point of access to a set of pods**. To create a service, another configuration file (`service.yaml`) is all we need.

```
apiVersion: v1
kind: Service
metadata:
    name: deep-learning-production-service
spec:
    type: LoadBalancer
    selector:
    app: deep-learning-production
    ports:
        - port: 80
    targetPort: 8080
```

As you can see, we declare a new Service of type load balancer which targets all pods (the `selector` field) with the name "deep-learning-production". It also exposes the 80 port and maps it to the 8080 target port of our pods (which we defined before, in the `deployment.yaml` file).

We apply the config:

```
$ kubectl apply -f service.yaml
```

And we get the status of our service:

```
$ kubectl get services
```

As we can observe below, the "deep-learning-production" service has been created and is exposed in an external IP through the predefined port.

```
NAME     TYPE     CLUSTER-IP  EXTERNAL-IP PORT(S) AGE
deep-learning-production    LoadBalancer    10.39.243.226
34.77.224.151   80:30159/TCP    75s
kubernetes  ClusterIP   10.39.240.1 <none>  443/TCP 35m
```

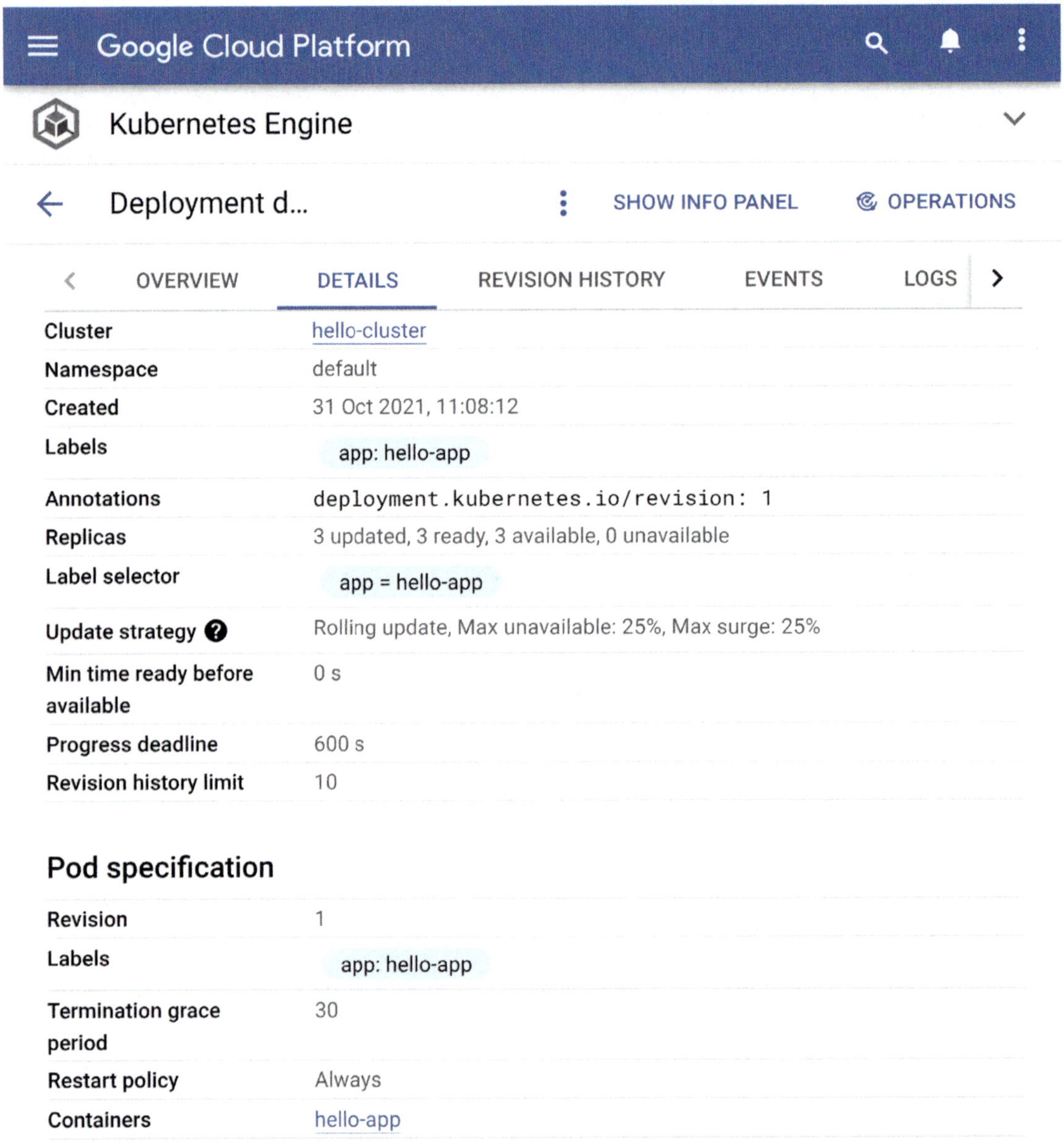

Figure 9.15: Deployments details in GKE dashboard

If we call this API with a client, we should get back a response from one of the pods containing the Tensorflow model. And in case you didn't notice, we just deployed our scalable application into the cloud.

The above steps will handle the creation of pods and all the networking between the different components and the external world.

Now you might wonder: Were all the above necessary? Couldn't we create a VM instance and push the container there? Wouldn't it be much simpler?

Maybe it would, to be honest. But the reason we chose Kubernetes is what comes after the deployment. Let's have a look around and see what benefits Kubernetes has and how it can help us grow the application as more users join. And most importantly: why is it especially useful for ML applications?

GKE gives us an easy way to manage everything. We can directly inspect all our services, our pods, the number of replicas, as well as some nice visualizations about CPU, memory and disk utilization. That way, we can be aware of our app performance at every time. But that's not all.

Let's explore some functionalities that GKE provides.

9.2.4 Scaling with Kubernetes

First of all, we can manually **scale the number of pods inside the Deployment**. For example: if we observe a big spike in the number of requests, we can increase the replicas. Note that the term replicas refers to a set of identical pods.

Therefore, the application's response time will gradually start to decline again. We can do that from the terminal using the `scale` command:

```
$ kubectl scale deployment DEPLOYMENT_NAME --replicas 4
```

So, we effortlessly solve scalability. As we grow, we can add more and more replicas hidden behind the service, which will handle all the load balancing and routing stuff.

If you played arounf with GKE, you might have also noticed that there is an autoscale button. That's right. **Kubernetes and GKE let us define autoscaling behaviour a priori**. We can instruct GKE to track a few metrics such as response time or request rate, and then increase the number of pods/replicas when they exceed a predefined threshold. Kubernetes supports two kinds of auto scaling:

- **Horizontal Pod Autoscaling (HPA)**
- **Vertical Pod Autoscaling (VPA)**

HPA creates new replicas to scale the application. In the below example, HPA targets the CPU utilization and autoscales when it becomes larger than 50%. Note that we need to define a minimum and a maximum number of replicas to keep things under control.

```
$ kubectl autoscale deployment DEPLOYMENT_NAME --cpu-percent=50
--min=1 --max=10
```

To track our HPA:

```
$ kubectl autoscale deployment DEPLOYMENT_NAME --cpu-percent=50
--min=1 --max=10

NAME    REFERENCE    TARGETS MINPODS MAXPODS REPLICAS    AGE
dlp Deployment/dlp  0%/50%  1    10  3    61s
```

In a similar manner we can configure VPA. VPA is scaling up the existing pods instead of scaling out. In my experience, HPA should be usually preferred.

9.2.5 Updating the application

When we want to update our application with a new Docker image (perhaps to use a new model, or a retrained one), we can perform a rolling update. A rolling update means that Kubernetes will gradually replace all the running pods one by one, with the new version. At the same time, it ensures that there will be no downfall in the performance. In the below example, we replace the Docker image with a newer version.

```
$ kubectl set image deployment dlp  dlp_image=dlp_image:2.0
```

9.2.6 Monitoring the application

In order to optimize our infrastructure and keep track of the model's accuracy, we also need to have some form of monitoring and logging. GKE has been automatically configured with Google Cloud's monitoring system. So, we can easily access all the logs.

If we click on the container logs inside a specific pod, we can navigate to "Cloud logging" and debug our app for errors.

Moreover, we have access to some cool visualizations and charts to help us monitor things better, as presented in the Figure 9.17.

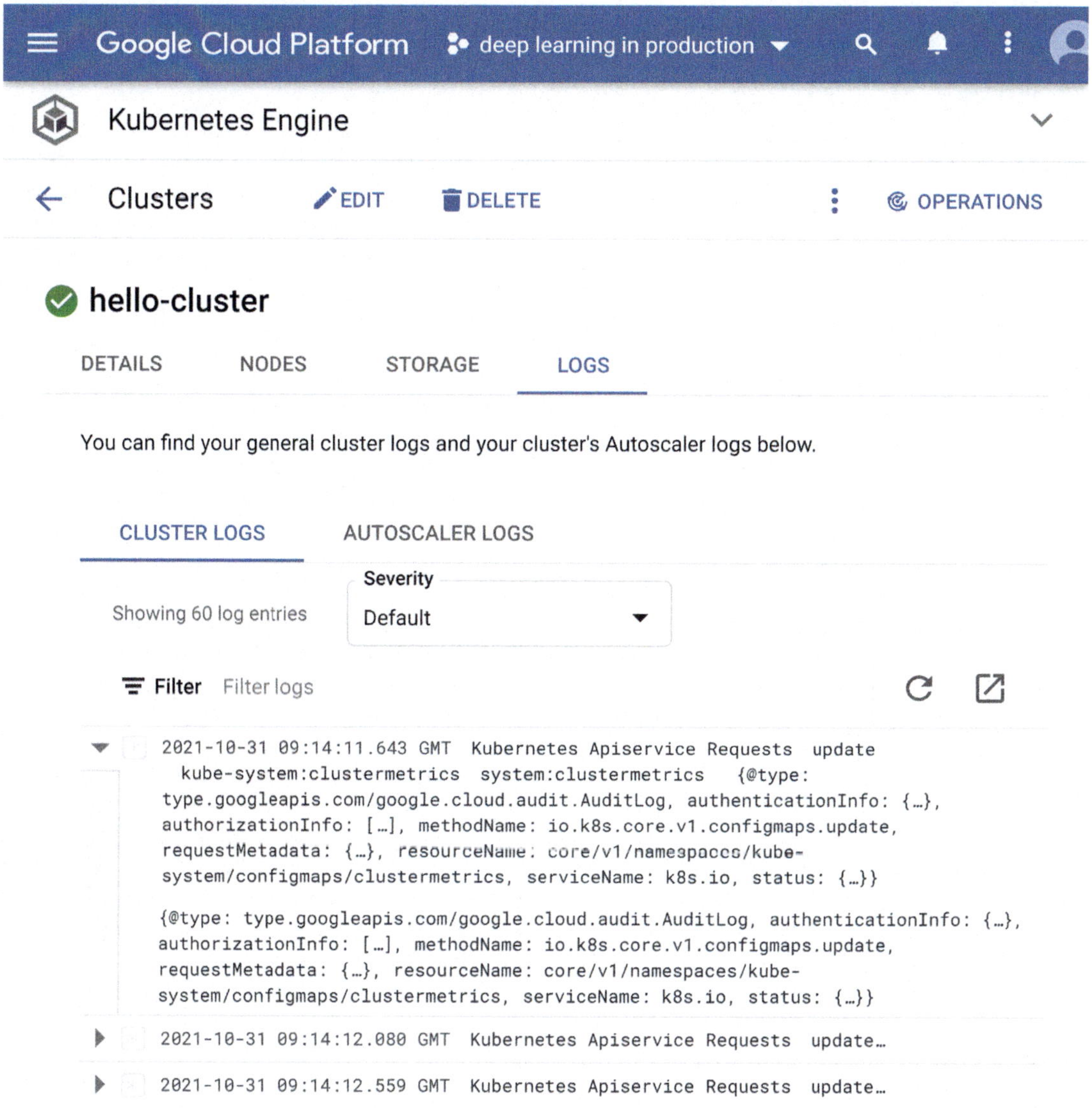

Figure 9.16: Logs in GKE

9.2.7 Running a (re)training job

Running jobs is another integral part of modern applications. In the case of ML, the most common example is a training job where we train (or retrain) our model in the cloud on a set of data. Again, with Kubernetes, it becomes just another yaml file (`train-job.yaml`). An example config will look like this:

Figure 9.17: Google Kubernetes engine dashboard

```
apiVersion: batch/v1
kind: Job
metadata:
    name: train-job
spec:
    template:
        metadata:
            name: train-job
    spec:
        containers:
            - name: train-dlp
            image: training_image
            command: ["python"]
            args: ["train.py", "-model", "unet", "-data",
            "gs://deep-learning-in-prodiction-training-data
                /oxford_iiit_pet/"]
        restartPolicy: Never
    backoffLimit: 4
```

Once we apply the config file, Kubernetes will spin up the necessary pods and run the job.

```
$ kubectl apply -f train-job.yaml
```

We can even configure things such as parallelism and number of retries after failures. Refer to the official docs for more on this subject.

9.2.8 Using Kubernetes with GPUs

Deep learning without GPUs is like ice cream with low fat milk (decent but not awesome). To use Kubernetes with GPUs, all we have to do is:

- Create nodes equipped with NVIDIA GPUs
- Install the necessary drivers
- Install the CUDA library
- Modify our Tensorflow code to use GPUs

Everything else will stay exactly the same. Adding GPUs to an existing cluster might be a little trickier than creating a new one, but again, the official recommendation has everything we need.

9.2.9 Model A/B testing

Another common deep learning-specific use case is model A/B testing. A/B testing refers to running multiple versions of the same model simultaneously. By doing that, we can keep track of which model performs better and keep only the best ones in production. There are several ways to accomplish that, using Kubernetes. Here is what I'd personally do:

I would create a separate Service and Deployment to host the second version of the model, and I would hide both services behind an external load balancer (or an Ingress as Kubernetes calls it).

The first part is exactly what we did before. The second part is slightly more difficult. In this direction, let's make some remarks.

In a nutshell, **an Ingress object defines a set of rules for routing HTTP traffic inside a cluster**. An Ingress object is associated with one or more Service objects, with each one associated with a set of pods. Under the hood, it is effectively a load balancer, with all the standard load balancing features (single point of entrance, authentication, and well... load balancing)

To create an Ingress object, we should build a new config file (`ingress.yaml`) with a structure as the one that follows:

```yaml
apiVersion: networking.k8s.io/v1
kind: Ingress
metadata:
    name: dlp-ingress
spec:
    rules:
        - http:
            paths:
                - path: /model1
                backend:
                    serviceName: model1
                    servicePort: 8080
                - path: /model2
                backend:
                    serviceName: model2
                    servicePort: 8081
```

As usual, we can integrate the Ingress using the `apply` command.

```
$ kubectl apply -f ingress.yaml
```

The Ingress load balancer will route the requests on the different services based on the path of the request. All requests coming in the `/model1` endpoint will be served by the first service and all requests on `/model2` by the second service. This is called "Fanout" in engineering terms.

And that officially ends our journey in Kubernetes, GKE and scalability.

Chapter 10

Building an End-to-End Pipeline

In this chapter:

- What is MLOps
- How to build a pipeline with Tensorflow Extended
- How to use Vertex AI in Google Cloud

In this chapter, we will present the basic principles behind MLOps and how it aims to standardize ML infrastructure. We will see some examples of MLOps frameworks that tackle the entire ML pipeline and we will explore a practical example with Tensorflow Extended (TFX). We will also make a tour of Google Cloud's MLOps solution, called Vertex AI.

10.1 MLOps

In recent years, there has been an effort from tech companies and the open-source community to try and standardize the entire ML workflow. The goal is to build end-to-end tools that cover every aspect of the ML pipeline, from prototyping to deployment. The term we most often use to describe this endeavour is "MLOps".

MLOps is the extension of the DevOps methodology to include ML and

Data Science assets as first-class citizens within the DevOps ecosystem.

MLOps has some key goals:

- To increase **automation** in ML.
- To enable **communication** and collaboration between data scientists, ML engineers, and DevOps engineers.
- To enable easy **experimentation** and **testing**.
- To provide **observability**and monitoring capabilities.
- To make ML **reproducible**.

10.1.1 Basic principles

To meet these goals, we first need to define a few core design principles. Every MLOps tool or software should be:

- **Versatile**: Due to the vast variety of ML frameworks and libraries, we need to support every major ML framework and make the tool language/library agnostic. This also entails that functionalities such as GPU training, distributed training, online-offline inference, batch inference should be also supported.
- **Scalable**: Of course, we want it to be as horizontally and vertically scalable as possible, meaning that both big amounts of data and very large models are supported.
- **Seamless**: Prototyping, data engineering, deployment and every step of the pipeline should be as easy to use as possible.

And similarly with any large-scale software system, it needs to be highly maintainable, extensible, reliable, and always available.

10.1.2 MLOps levels

Building an ML infrastructure system is by no means a one-off task and requires careful planning and different iteration steps. The Google Cloud blog defines 3 basic levels of iteration:

Level 0: Manual process

In the beginning, building and deploying ML models requires lot of manual work. Below is a typical example:

1. Engineers and Data scientists extract and load the data using one-off scripts and queries.

2. Model prototypes are developed and trained locally in Jupyter notebooks or IDEs.
3. A trained model is then passed to the backend teams, who optimize it, package it, and usually store it in a model registry.
4. DevOps engineers then deploy it manually in production.

While this process definitely works, it has some serious drawbacks:

- It doesn't allow rapid experimentation and frequent retraining.
- Monitoring the model performance is not always easy.
- Lots of hand-written scripts and code need to be developed and executed each time.

Level 1: ML pipeline automation

As the team grows and more models are starting to be developed, automation is slowly being added into the mix. This enables easy deployment of new models and fast retraining of existing ones. But how?

To automate data extraction and transformation, data pipelines (distributed or not) are put in place. A typical example will look like this:

1. The data scientist loads the data from a feature store, database or data warehouse using flexible data querying tools.
2. The data scientist validates and cleans the data.
3. The model is trained either locally or in the cloud on the refined data
4. The model is then automatically verified, versioned and pushed into a model registry.
5. Deployments, like every step of the pipeline, can now be triggered automatically.

Key characteristics of this workflow are:

- Fast experimentation
- Testing and validation
- Lots of hand-written scripts and code need to be developed and executed each time
- Fast experimentation
- Testing and validation

- Decoupled and extensible components
- Monitoring
- Versioning
- Retraining of models in production

To sum up, in level 1 we can deploy new implementations of components and we can seamlessly integrate new data and new models. Why? Because we usually deal with only a few pipelines. In most cases, these pipelines are manually tested and deployed. But what about entirely new ML problems and applications? What if we wanted to experiment with different pipeline setups and environments?

Level 2: CI/CD pipeline automation

A mature MLOps project should make it easy for engineers to try out new pipelines, new serving environments, new data sources, and ML solutions. To accomplish that, pipelines should be handled by a Continuous Integration and Deployment (CI/CD) framework.

In order to be able to combine different components into different pipelines, we will most likely need an orchestrator as well. An orchestrator will be responsible for scheduling the execution of different components, monitoring each step of the pipeline and tying everything together.

A workflow example will be like this:

1. An ML Engineer wants to experiment with a fresh new idea.
2. The ML Engineer develops a new pipeline from scratch with all the different components. Everything from the data source to the production environment is left to their discretion.
3. The ML Engineer deploys, debugs the pipeline and analyses the results. If they are promising, the engineer iteratively builds upon it. If not, it's time for something new.

Key characteristics:

- Rapid prototyping of novel ML ideas and pipelines
- High automation in every step of the way
- Seamless integration of new models, data, code

10.2 Building a pipeline using TFX

So far in this book, we examined every part of the ML lifecycle as an independent component. We looked at data pre-processing, training, serving, deployment, scalability, all as a standalone problem that we need to solve. Pipelines exist to glue everything together and establish a singular and automated workflow. We no longer care only about training and deployment as individual entities. Instead, we care about how training and deployment interact with each other. That's why from now on, we will think in terms of pipelines. A pipeline can, of course, take advantage of all the libraries and tools we talked about so far, such as Flask, uWSGI, Docker, Kubernetes. All have their place here. The difference is how we integrate them to form a pipeline. Towards that goal, one can adopt tools such as Tensorflow Extended.

TensorFlow Extended (TFX) is an end-to-end platform for deploying production ML pipelines. It's developed by Google and as the name suggests, it is based on Tensorflow. TFX tries to abstract all different parts of the pipeline and provide ready-to-use components with minimal boilerplate code. Its main purpose is to alleviate the technical debt that comes with ML systems.

10.2.1 TFX glossary

Components are the building blocks of a pipeline and are the ones that perform all the work.

Metadata store is a single source of truth for all components. It contains 3 things basically:

- Artifacts and their properties: these can be trained models, data, metrics etc.
- Execution records of components and pipelines.
- Metadata about the workflow (order of components, inputs, outputs etc).

TFX pipeline is a portable implementation of an ML workflow that is composed of component instances and input parameters.

Orchestrators are systems that execute TFX pipelines. They are basically platforms to author, schedule and monitor workflows. They usually represent a pipeline as a Directed Acyclic Graph (DAG) and make sure that each job (or worker) is executed at the correct time with the correct input. Examples of popular orchestrators that work with TFX are Apache Airflow, Apache Beam, and Kubeflow pipelines.

Based on the different stages of the ML lifecycle, TFX provides a set of different components with standard functionality. These components can of course be overridden if we want to extend their functionality, or they can be replaced by entirely new ones.

In most cases, though, the built-in components will take us a long way down the road.

Let's do a quick walk-through on some of them, starting with data loading and ending with deployment. Note that we will not analyze every single line of the code because there are a lot of new libraries and packages. The point is to give you an overview of TFX and its modules, so as to understand why we need such end-to-end solutions.

Note that, in the following code snippets, we will use a set of predefined components. However, TFX is flexible enough so that we can create and use new components. One can take their existing code, package it as a standalone TFX component and integrate it in their pipeline, without having to rely on the components provided by the library.

10.2.2 Data ingestion

The first phase of the ML development process is data loading. The `ExampleGen` component ingests data into a TFX pipeline by converting different types of data to `tf.Record` or `tf.Example` (both supported by TFX). Sample code can be found below:

```
from tfx.proto import example_gen_pb2
from tfx.components import ImportExampleGen

input_config = example_gen_pb2.Input(splits=[
     example_gen_pb2.Input.Split(name='train', pattern='train/*'),
     example_gen_pb2.Input.Split(name='eval', pattern='test/*')
 ])

example_gen = ImportExampleGen(
     input_base=data_root, input_config=input_config
)
```

`ImportExampleGen` is a special type of `ExampleGen` that receives a data path and a configuration on how to handle the data. In this case, we split them into training and test datasets.

Note that `ImportExampleGen` is not the only alternative. A better approach is to take our existing code that we developed in Chapter 5, package it as a TFX component and use it in the pipeline. That way, we can take advantage of `tf.data` and all the tools we used.

10.2.3 Data validation

The next step is to explore, visualize and validate our data for possible inaccuracies and anomalies.

The `StatisticsGen` component generates a set of useful statistics describing our data distribution. As you can see, it receives the output of `ExampleGen`:

```
from tfx.components import StatisticsGen

statistics_gen =
    StatisticsGen(examples=example_gen.outputs['examples'])
```

`Tensorflow Data Validation` is a built-in TFX library that, among other things, can help us visualize the statistics produced by `StatisticsGen`. It is used internally by `StatisticsGen` but can also be used as a stand-alone tool.

```
import tensorflow_data_validation as tfdv

tfdv.visualize_statistics(stats)
```

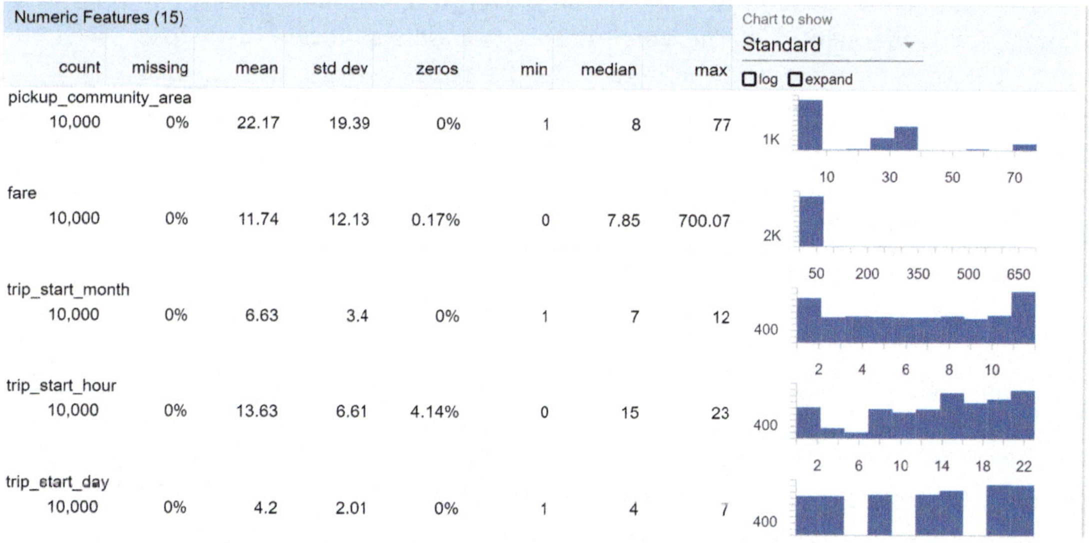

Figure 10.1: Tensorflow data validation example

The same library is being used by `SchemaGen`, which generates a primitive schema for our data. This can be of course adjusted based on our domain knowledge, but it is a decent starting point.

```python
from tfx.components import SchemaGen

schema_gen = SchemaGen(
      statistics=statistics_gen.outputs['statistics'],
      infer_feature_shape=True
     )
```

The schema and statistics produced can now be utilized in order to perform some form of data validation that will catch outliers, anomalies and errors in our dataset.

```python
from tfx.components import ExampleValidator

example_validator = ExampleValidator(
      statistics=statistics_gen.outputs['statistics'],
      schema=schema_gen.outputs['schema'])
```

10.2.4 Feature engineering

One of the most important steps in any ML pipeline is feature engineering, where we pre-process our data so that it can be passed into our model. TFX provides the `Transform` component and the `tensorflow_transform` library to help us with the task. The transform step can be performed like this:

```python
from tfx.components import Transform

transform = Transform(
      examples=example_gen.outputs['examples'],
      schema=schema_gen.outputs['schema'],
      module_file=module_file)
```

But that's not the whole story. We need to define our pre-processing functionality somehow. This is where the argument `module_file` comes in. The most usual way to do that is to have a different file with all our transformations. The key thing is that we need to implement a `preprocessing_fn` function which is the point of entrance for TFX. Here is a sample:

```python
def preprocessing_fn(inputs):
   """tf.transform's callback function for preprocessing inputs."""
   outputs = {}

   image_features = tf.map_fn(
```

```
        lambda x: tf.io.decode_png(x[0], channels=3),
        inputs[_IMAGE_KEY],
        dtype=tf.uint8
    )
    image_features = tf.cast(image_features, tf.float32)
    image_features = tf.image.resize(image_features, [224, 224])
    image_features = tf.keras.applications.mobilenet.preprocess_input(
        image_features)

    outputs[_transformed_name(_IMAGE_KEY)] = image_features
    outputs[_transformed_name(_LABEL_KEY)] = inputs[_LABEL_KEY]

    return outputs
```

As you can see, it is normal Tensorflow and Keras code.

10.2.5 Train the model

In contrast to what many people believe, training is not a one-time operation. Models need to be retrained constantly to stay relevant and ensure the best possible accuracy in their results.

```
from tfx.dsl.components.base import executor_spec
from tfx.proto import trainer_pb2
from tfx.components.trainer.executor import GenericExecutor
from tfx.components import Trainer

 trainer = Trainer(
      module_file=module_file,
      custom_executor_spec=
        executor_spec.ExecutorClassSpec(GenericExecutor),
      examples=transform.outputs['transformed_examples'],
      transform_graph=transform.outputs['transform_graph'],
      schema=schema_gen.outputs['schema'],
      train_args=trainer_pb2.TrainArgs(num_steps=160),
      eval_args=trainer_pb2.EvalArgs(num_steps=4),
      custom_config={'labels_path': labels_path})
```

As before, the training logic is in a separate module file. This time, we have to implement the `run_fn` function, which normally defines the model and training loop. Here is an example:

```python
def run_fn(fn_args: FnArgs):

  tf_transform_output =
    tft.TFTransformOutput(fn_args.transform_output)

  train_dataset = _input_fn(
      fn_args.train_files,
      tf_transform_output,
      is_train=True,
      batch_size=_TRAIN_BATCH_SIZE)
  eval_dataset = _input_fn(
      fn_args.eval_files,
      tf_transform_output,
      is_train=False,
      batch_size=_EVAL_BATCH_SIZE)

  model, base_model = _build_keras_model()

  model.compile(
      loss='sparse_categorical_crossentropy',
      optimizer=
        tf.keras.optimizers.RMSprop(lr=_FINETUNE_LEARNING_RATE),
      metrics=['sparse_categorical_accuracy'])
  model.summary(print_fn=absl.logging.info)

  model.fit(
      train_dataset,
      epochs=_CLASSIFIER_EPOCHS,
      steps_per_epoch=steps_per_epoch,
      validation_data=eval_dataset,
      validation_steps=fn_args.eval_steps,
      callbacks=[tensorboard_callback])
```

Note that the `_build_keras_model` returns a vanilla `tf.keras.Sequential` model, while `input_fn` returns a batched dataset of training examples and labels. Also be sure that with the correct callbacks, we can take advantage of Tensorboard to visualize the training progress.

Once again, everything that we talked about in Chapter 6 still applies. We can utilize the cloud to train the model, we can take advantage of distributed training and so on. The difference is that everything is self-contained inside a TFX component that integrates seamlessly with other components inside the pipeline.

10.2.6 Validate model

Once we train a model, we should evaluate it and analyse its performance before we push it into production. TensorFlow Model Analysis (TFMA) is a library for that purpose. Notice here that the actual model evaluation has already happened during training. This step intends to record evaluation metrics for future runs and compare it with previous models. That way, we can be sure that our current model is the best we have at the moment.

I will not go into the details of TFMA but here is some code for future reference. We need to create an evaluation config where we define the different tasks the `Evaluator` will conduct. This config is subsequently passed in the `tfx.Evaluator` method.

```
import tensorflow_model_analysis as tfma

eval_config = tfma.EvalConfig(
      model_specs=[tfma.ModelSpec(label_key='label_xf',
          model_type='tf_lite')
      ],
      slicing_specs=[tfma.SlicingSpec()],
      metrics_specs=[
          tfma.MetricsSpec(metrics=[
              tfma.MetricConfig(
                  class_name='SparseCategoricalAccuracy',
                  threshold=tfma.MetricThreshold(
                      value_threshold=tfma.GenericValueThreshold(
                          lower_bound={'value': 0.55}),
                      change_threshold=tfma.GenericChangeThreshold(
                          direction=
                            tfma.MetricDirection.HIGHER_IS_BETTER,
                          absolute={'value': -1e-3}))
          ])
      ])
```

The important part is where we define our `Evaluator` component as a part of our pipeline.

```
from tfx.components import Evaluator
```

```
evaluator = Evaluator(
      examples=transform.outputs['transformed_examples'],
      model=trainer.outputs['model'],
      baseline_model=model_resolver.outputs['model'],
      eval_config=eval_config)
```

10.2.7 Push model

Once the model validation succeeds, it's time to push the model into production. This is the job of the Pusher component, which handles all the deploying stuff depending on our environment.

```
from tfx.components import Pusher

 pusher = Pusher(
      model=trainer.outputs['model'],
      model_blessing=evaluator.outputs['blessing'],
      push_destination=pusher_pb2.PushDestination(
          filesystem=pusher_pb2.PushDestination.Filesystem(
              base_directory=serving_model_dir)))
```

What's the deployment target here? Because we used the built-in Pusher component, the model will be served with Tensorflow Serving. Does that mean that all the work we did with Flask, uWSGI, Docker and Kubernetes is wasted?

The beauty of MLOps tools such as TFX is that they are library-agnostic. That's why we can replace the built-in components with our own. We can wrap the model in a Flask/uWSGI application, containerize it with Docker and push it to Kubernetes. All that could be included in a standalone TFX component. And even better, we can plug a different TFX component for each model's pipeline, depending on the application needs.

10.2.8 Build a TFX pipeline

So far, we defined a number of components so far that contain everything we need. But how do we tie them together? TFX pipelines are defined using the Pipeline class, which receives a list of components among other things.

```
from tfx.orchestration import metadata
from tfx.orchestration import pipeline

  components = [
```

```
    example_gen, statistics_gen, schema_gen, example_validator,
    transform, trainer, model_resolver, evaluator, pusher
]

pipeline = pipeline.Pipeline(
    pipeline_name=pipeline_name,
    pipeline_root=pipeline_root,
    components=components,
    enable_cache=True)
```

Component instances produce artifacts (i.e. models, data, metrics) as outputs and typically depend on artifacts produced by upstream component instances as inputs. The order of execution of the components is determined by a Directed Acyclic Graph (DAG) based on each artifact's dependencies. A typical TFX pipeline can be found in the Figure 10.2.

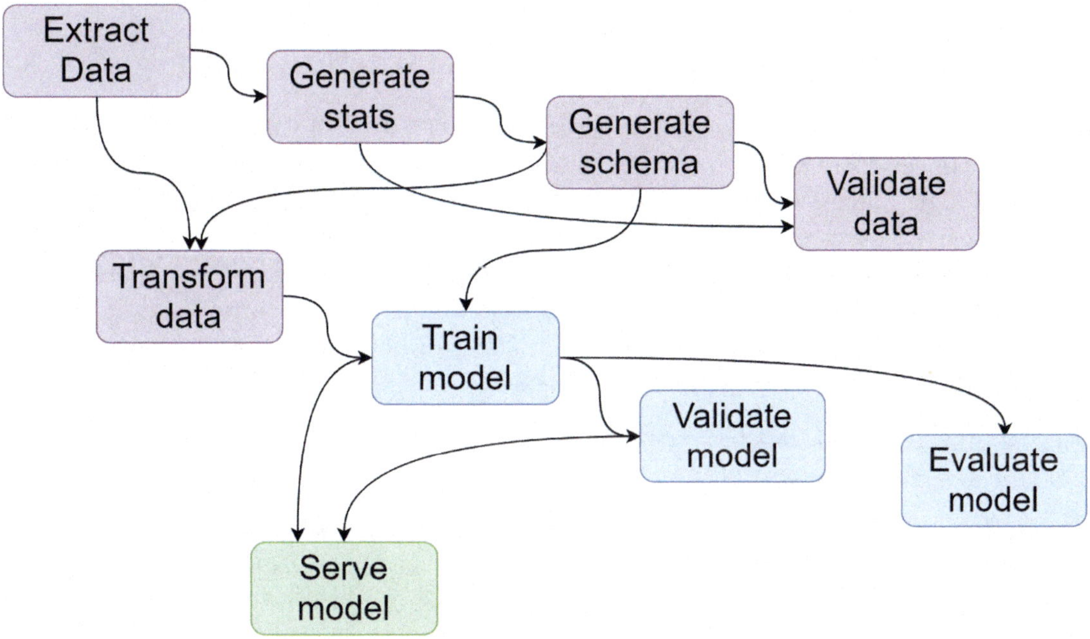

Figure 10.2: A sample TFX pipeline

10.2.9 Run a TFX pipeline

At last, we reach the part where we will run the pipeline. To do so we need an orchestrator. Pipelines are executed by an orchestrator, which will handle all the job scheduling and networking. Here I chose Apache Beam using `BeamDagRunner`, but the same principles are true for Kubeflow or Airflow.

```
from tfx.orchestration.beam.beam_dag_runner import BeamDagRunner

if __name__ == '__main__':
    BeamDagRunner().run( pipeline)
```

If needed, similar commands can be executed from the command line using the TFX CLI.

Typically, orchestrators like Apache Beam will run on cloud resources. This means that depending on the environment and the pipeline, Beam will spin up cloud instances/workers and stream data through them. Commonly-used orchestrators apart from Apache Beam include Spark, Flink, Google Dataflow. On the other hand, orchestrators like Kubeflow rely on Kubernetes. It turns out that one important job of MLOps engineers is finding the best environment for their needs.

10.3 MLOps with Vertex AI and Google Cloud

In many cases, pipeline automation with tools like TFX is all we ever need. However there are times where we might want to use a more hands-off approach. Companies such as Google and AWS, have built MLOps platforms that aim to unify all machine learning-related services under a single umbrella. One such platform is Vertex AI. Vertex AI is GCP's MLOps solution and it combines training and prediction services with AutoML, data labelling and explainable AI (XAI) components of Google Cloud. Vertex AI can be added on top of TFX or can be utilized without any pipeline automation tool, depeding on the project needs.

On the other hand, it can be very opinionated and it removes the control from the hands of the MLOps engineers.

Vertex AI and similar solutions can undoubtedly simplify ML operations on a large scale. Does that mean though that they should be considered as panacea? The truth is that in many applications, Vertex AI can be an ideal solution because it minimizes the time between prototyping and deployment. It has a minimal overhead and allows us to not have to worry at all about Flask, Docker, Kubernetes etc. Everything is being taken care of behind the scenes, and we are free to focus only on the actual ML part of the lifecycle. However, someone might argue that these solutions remove the control from the hands of engineers for the sake of simplicity and productivity. They can be seen as black boxes where everything is handled by the cloud providers, leaving minimal flexibility to the team.

Why use Vertex AI?

- Fast experimentation and deployment are a must
- Zero configuration
- Minimal DevOps background in the team
- No advanced and custom infrastructure needs
- Repeatability
- Easy scaling and maintenance
- No steep learning curve
- Ideal for beginners
- Minimal overhead

Why not use Vertex AI?

- Vertex AI is more expensive than standard compute engine instances or GKE
- Limited control over deployment and serving
- Cloud vendor lock in
- Closed-source solutions
- Highly opinionated

Let's have a closer look at the different functionalities of Vertex AI. Following the standard ML lifecycle, one can utilize Vertex AI to:

1. Define and upload a dataset to train a model.
2. Experiment with jupyter notebooks directly in the cloud.
3. Manage feature data in low-latency feature stores.
4. Train models using custom training code or AutoML.
5. Evaluate the model and tune its hyperparameters.
6. Build data labelling jobs where one can request human labelling on the data.
7. Upload and store multiple models with a versioning system.
8. Deploy the model and get an endpoint for serving predictions.
9. Design and deploy pipelines that cover the entire lifecycle.
10. Manage the different models and endpoints.

On top of all that, one can further take advantage of all the other available GCP services such as logging, monitoring, error reporting and so on.

At this point, I think it's best to integrate all the above into our own project to showcase the strengths and weaknesses of MLOps. To do that, we need to disregard everything we did over the past chapters regarding serving, deployment and scalability. We will keep only the vanilla form of our application containing the training and prediction code. So, no more Flask, uWSGI, Nginx and Kubernetes. That's because Vertex AI will handle all the infrastructure for us.

10.3.1 Hands on Vertex AI

In order to get started with Vertex AI, we should have created a GCP project as we discussed in the previous chapters. Afterwards, we should enable the Vertex AI API so we can access all Vertex AI's functionalities. Once everything is in place, we can inspect the dedicated dashboard. It should look like the Figure 10.3:

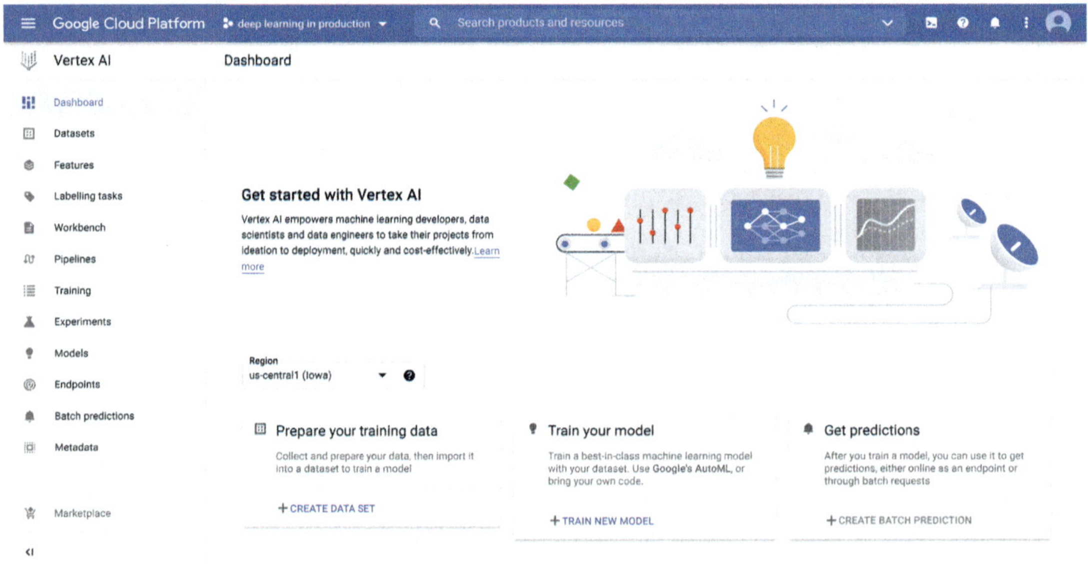

Figure 10.3: Vertex AI dashboard

We can also observe the different services in the left sidebar as usual. At the time of writing this book, we have the components as shown in the table below:

Vertex AI Services	Functionality
Datasets	Dataset management and labeling
Features	Feature stores
Labeling tasks	Outsourcing labeling jobs
Workbench	Notebook environments
Pipelines	Pipelining (TFX etc.)
Training	Model training (AutoML included)
Experiments	ML experiements comparison (Tensorboard)
Models	Management of trained models
Endpoints	Endpoints of deployed models
Batch predictions	Batch predictions for bulk scoring
Metadata	Manage metadata and data lineage
Vizier	Hyperparameter optimization

Following the MLOps principles, Vertex AI aims to be an all-in-one solution that streamlines the entire ML lifecycle. Let's see how it accomplishes this.

10.3.2 Experimenting with notebooks

First of all, Vertex AI can play an important role during the experimentation phase of ML. One can create and run jupyter notebooks directly on the cloud rather than a local environment. Once we create a new notebook, a dedicated VM instance is being assigned to it. The notebook's code will execute directly on the instance. That way, we don't have to worry about setting up the environment ourselves. Notebook instances have `JupyterLab` pre-installed and are configured with GPU-enabled ML frameworks. On top of that, we can also install additional dependencies and persist our notebooks with git and Github.

10.3.3 Loading data

Regarding data, there are two main choices when it comes to Vertex AI.

1. Use a managed dataset

2. Use a third-party data loading system

Managed Datasets

Vertex AI lets us create Dataset objects that can be used for AutoML or custom training. A managed dataset should correspond to one of the predefined data types and objectives, as shown in the Figure 10.5. In our case, we can select the "image segmentation" option from the "images" tab. We will also need to select an annotation type, based on the types of labels we use.

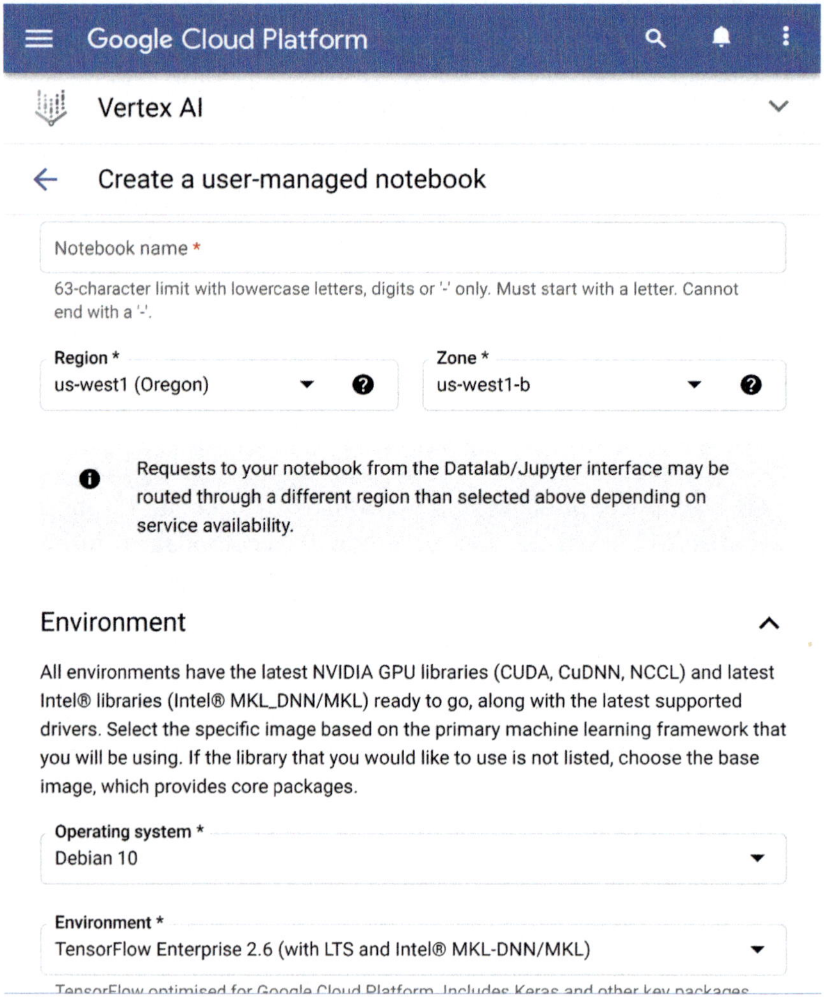

Figure 10.4: Notebook creation on Vertex AI

The data can be imported from a local folder or a cloud storage object. Once they are ready, we can browse each individual image, analyse them, examine their statistics, split them into training and test datasets, and more. We can also create labelling tasks if it is necessary. Behind the scenes, the data is stored inside a bucket in cloud storage.

One thing that we should take into consideration is that Vertex AI has its own rules for importing data depending on the task at hand. For example, if we have unlabelled data, we need to provide only the images, while for labelled data, a schema with the data structure is also required. Here, we won't go into details on how to prepare the data for import because it depends on the task. As always, the official documentation

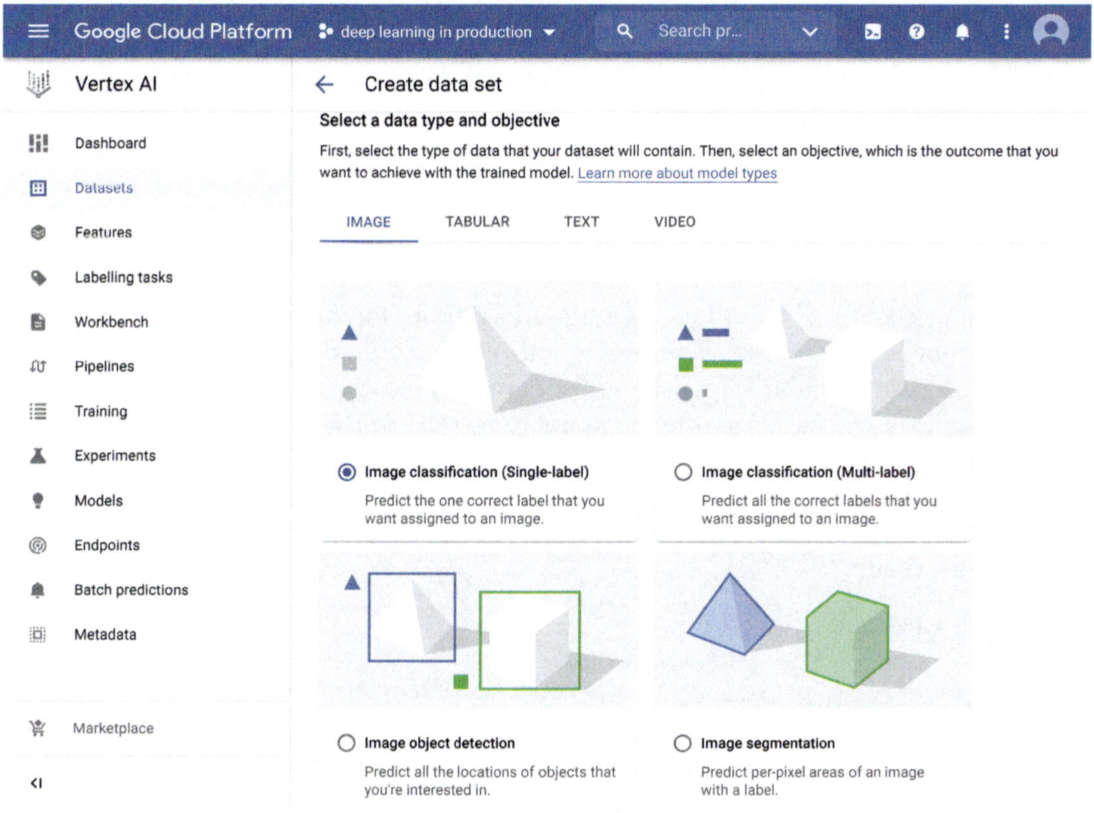

Figure 10.5: Vertex AI datasets

has everything you might need.

Custom datasets

On the other hand, we can choose to use our own data loading functionality. In that case, the data will be imported using `tfds`, `tf.data` or any other library. The disadvantage of that option is that we lose the ability to analyse and inspect the data inside Vertex AI. As a result, all data manipulation and cleaning should occur locally or in a cloud notebook.

For our application, we will use a custom dataset since our existing code already loads the data with `tfds`. An alternative way would be to upload the data in a bucket in Cloud storage and load it directly from there, as discussed in Chapter 6.2.

10.3.4 Training the model

Training the model is quite straightforward and can be achieved with a few clicks. First, we should define the training dataset. This can be a Vertex AI dataset, or we can choose to use a "no managed dataset". In our example, we will select "no managed dataset" because the data are loaded directly in the training loop using `tfds`. Next, we need to define a few model details (e.g name, version etc) and the training container.

The training container should contain all the training functionality. It can be a pre-built container from Vertex AI repository or our custom container. For our application, we can easily build a Docker image with only the data-loading and training code, and then upload the corresponding container. Note that the custom container should live in the GCP container registry.

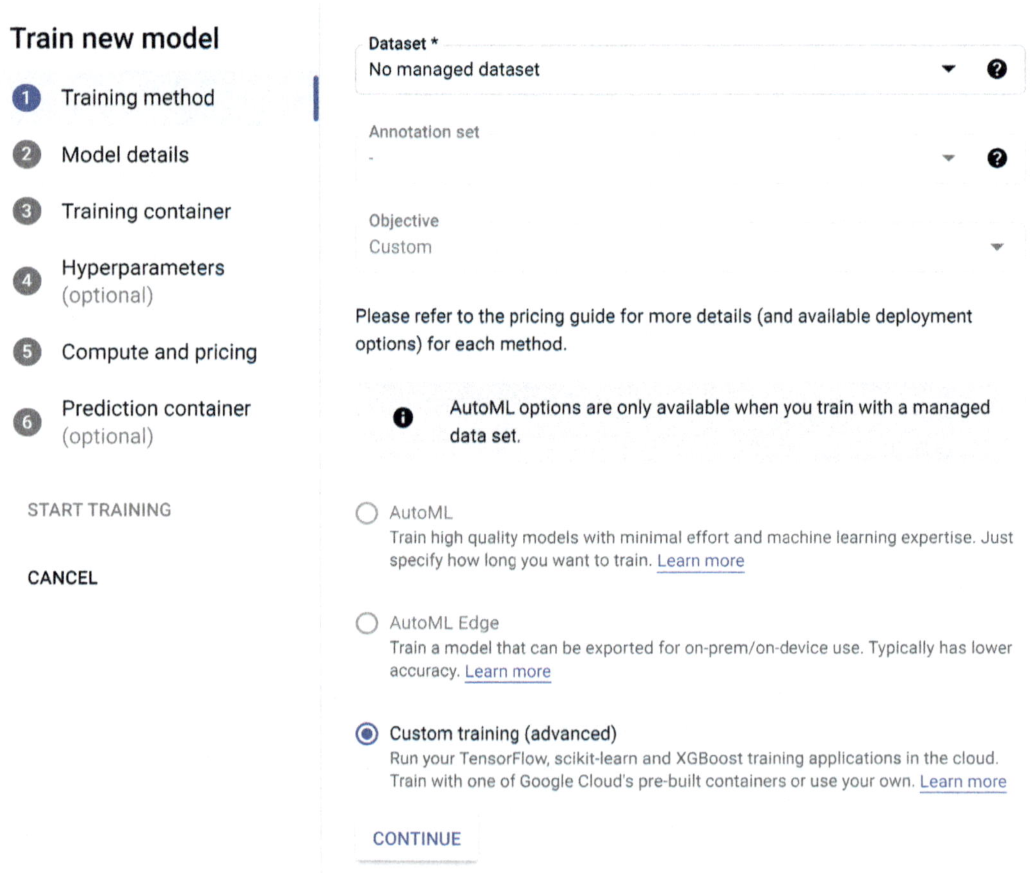

Figure 10.6: Training in Vertex AI

To do so, we can write a simple Dockerfile as below.

```
FROM tensorflow/tensorflow:nightly

WORKDIR /trainer

COPY trainer /trainer

RUN pip install -r requirements.txt
ENTRYPOINT ["python", "train.py"]
```

We simply copy all of our training code in the container, install the necessary dependencies and run the training script.

Once the image has been built, we need to push the container into the GCP container registry, so it can be accessed from other cloud services.

```
$ docker build ./ -t "vertex-ai-trainer"

$ docker tag vertex-ai-trainer
    gcr.io/deep-learning-in-production/vertex-ai-trainer

$ docker push "vertex-ai-trainer"
```

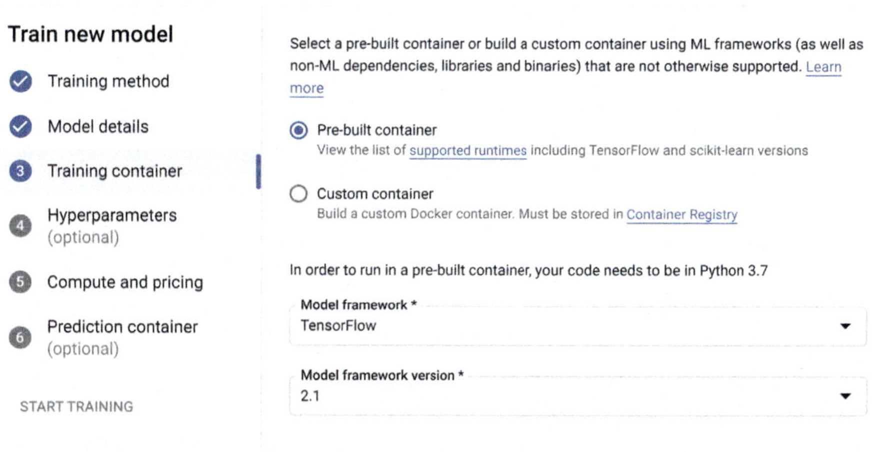

Figure 10.7: Training container selection on Vertex AI

Subsequently, we have a few more steps in order to start the training:

- We can optionally set up hyperparameter tuning

- We need to specify the computing resources for the training jobs
- We can optionally define a prediction container as well

If everything is set up correctly, the custom training pipeline will start immediately. During training, we can inspect the logs, monitor the accuracy, visualize the process with Tensorboard, etc. Note that trained model artifacts should be stored in cloud storage.

10.3.5 Deploying to Vertex AI

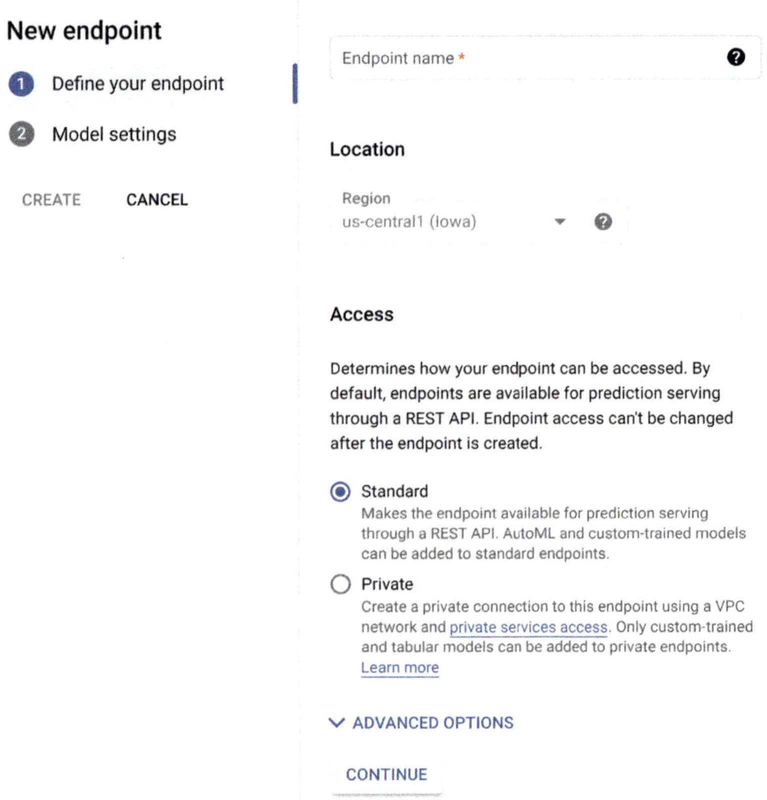

Figure 10.8: Endpoint creation on Vertex AI

When the training is complete, it's time for deployment. Vertex AI has two more entities related to deployment. A model and an endpoint.

Creating a model

A model is simply an artifact with the model weights and metadata. A model can be created after a training execution or can be imported from a cloud storage location.

In our case, it will be a `.pb` file with the UNet's weights that has been uploaded to a bucket after the completion of training.

Creating an endpoint

Once the model is initialized, we can create an endpoint that will serve the model's predictions. An endpoint associates a model with physical resources so it can be served online with low latency.

Besides online predictions, we can also configure batch predictions and traffic splitting for A/B testing between the new and older versions of the model. Moreover, Vertex AI takes care of load balancing, scaling, logging, monitoring, and security. That's the great thing about MLOps: it handles all the infrastructure for us, so we can dedicate our time to doing plain ML.

Once the endpoint is live, we can test it by sending an image for prediction using our client script or directly from the cloud console. If everything works correctly, we should see the segmentation mask of a Yorkshire terrier as usual.

10.3.6 Creating a pipeline

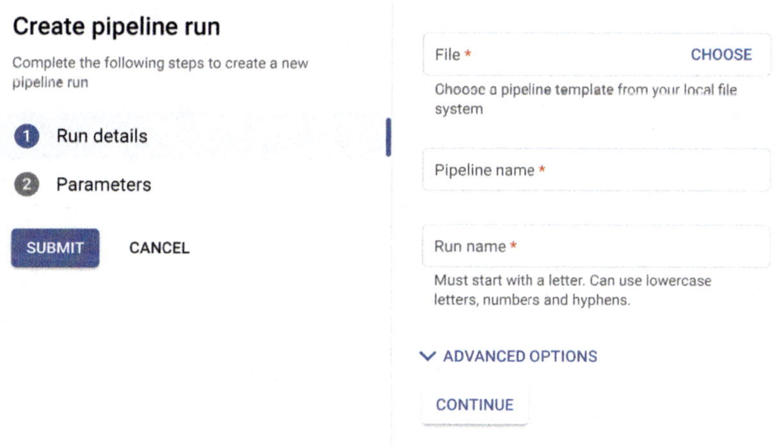

Figure 10.9: Pipeline creation on Vertex AI

What happens though if we don't only care about training and deployment? As we have extensively seen, the ML lifecycle consists of many more steps. Data statistics generation, data validation, testing, hyperparameter tuning, model evaluation, are only a few of them. This is where pipelines come into play. In the previous section, we saw how we can use TFX to build a collection of ML components that can be executed sequentially. Can we deploy this pipeline in Vertex AI? Absolutely. Vertex pipelines let us define, deploy and execute our own pipelines in Google Cloud.

In fact, we can take the TFX pipeline we developed in the previous section, and push it effortlessly in the cloud.

There are only two main differences that we should be aware of. First, we need to use the "Vertex ML Metadata" instead of TFX's metadata store. Secondly, we need to adjust the pipeline runner so it can be executed in GCP. A great option is to use the `KubeflowV2DagRunner`. This will set Kubeflow as the pipeline orchestrator and will execute all components on top of Kubernetes. This means that it can be integrated seamlessly with GCP infrastructure.

```
runner = tfx.orchestration.experimental.KubeflowV2DagRunner(
  config=tfx.orchestration.experimental.KubeflowV2DagRunnerConfig(),
  output_filename=PIPELINE_DEFINITION_FILE)
```

Once we do that, we can upload the `PIPELINE_DEFINITION_FILE` into Vertex and our TFX pipeline will be live and ready to be executed.

10.4 More end-to-end solutions

As a final section, I would like to present some of the most popular end-to-end solutions right now. MLOps is all about standardizing the ML lifecycle and building universal systems that anyone can incorporate into their applications. Which one should you choose for your own project depends heavily on your needs and requirements.

This decision is of high-importance and it should be carefully considered during the design phase of the lifecycle. The choice depends on the project's nature, the experience of the team, and the end goal of the application. As a result, careful research and experimentation is vital.

Since the MLOps landscape is changing rapidly, we won't dive into each one of them but be sure that all the principles we talked about in this book apply to most of them as well. Note that because these platforms are continually evolving in features and market positioning, we won't dive into details for each one of them. I will categorize them based on their key characteristics. Shall we begin?

MLOps from big cloud providers

In the same category with GCP's Vertex AI, you will also find AWS Sagemaker and Microsoft Azure Machine Learning. These are all-in-one solutions backed by the biggest companies in the tech industry. They contain a huge variety of services and provide everything you might need; from training and prediction endpoints to AutoML, data labeling and Explainable AI.

In my opinion, they should be preferred if there is little to non-existing backend background in the team. They can make deployment and MLOps trivial and they are perfect for beginners and ML researchers. However note that these are proprietary, expensive solutions and it might be difficult to migrate to a different platform in the future.

Open-source frameworks for ML workflows

On the other hand, one might prefer an open-source approach where they have total control over the infrastructure and they are not locked-in in a specific cloud vendor. In this category, you can find libraries such as Kubeflow, Metaflow, MLFlow, Flyte, Kedro or Seldon Core. Some of them actually begun as in-house solutions from big organizations but were later open-sourced. Others are open-source projects that have been evolved into fully-fledged frameworks.

In the same category, you can also find libraries such as Pachyderm or Data Version Control (DVC) that provide version control systems for management and versioning of datasets and ML models.

Each one has a unique set of characteristics and one should dive into their documentation and intricacies in order to fully utilize them. So they are most suitable for experienced engineers and bigger teams that want control and extensibility.

Enterprise solutions

Another option might be to use an enterprise framework that offers a more hands-off approach such as Algorithmia, Domino Data Lab, Daitaku, Datarobot and Valohai. While some might be more specialized than others, they usually come with advanced features, many automations, good developer support and different pricing plans.

Smaller but equally capable frameworks include cnvrg.io, Iguazio and allegro.ai. These are backed by smaller teams so they might miss a few features or lack customizability. But they can be quite cheaper and easy-to-use.

Enterprise frameworks can be an excellent choice when the team has adequate budget, not enough infrastructure experience and a specific need that is fulfilled by the corresponding library.

So how do I choose?

This final decision can be quite tricky but here are my two cents. It all depends on a number of questions that you need to ask. Depending on the answer, you might include or disregard a few options.

1. Do I want to use a CLI or a GUI approach?
2. Do I need support for all ML frameworks or just the popular ones?
3. Do I intend to use more standard Data Science approaches or Deep Learning?
4. Do I have experience in developing and maintaining infrastructure?
5. Do I want a more specialized approach that focuses on a particular MLOps task or an all-in solution?
6. How much can I afford?
7. Do I need good developer support?
8. Do I care more about the experimentation phase of ML or productization?
9. Do I need a highly experienced team maintaining my systems for me?
10. Do I need a high variety of services such as AutoML and XAI?
11. How much control do I want over my systems?
12. How much scalability do I need?
13. How much automation do I need?

As you understand, these questions don't always have a clear answer. That's why it's imperative to do good research and allocate a good portion of your time in designing the system beforehand. No matter the final choice, make sure to document your thoughts and analyze the pros/cons on a proper design doc. It will be beneficial both for the team and yourself in the future.

One final thing that I want to point out is that, while choosing the "best" tool is undoubtedly significant, making a decision is not always final. Following best practices and expanding upon the original software can sometimes compensate for an "imperfect" tool. And, of course, one can always migrate if they find that the technical debt is too high.

Chapter 11

Where to Go from Here

We finally did it. It's been a long journey, but I hope it was worth it. Developing deep learning applications is a continuous and complicated process that involves many different teams and engineers. From data processing and training to deployment and scaling, every part of the pipeline requires different software skills, frameworks and libraries.

In this book, we deliberately picked a handful of frameworks to explain things better and to give you concrete examples, but ultimately the choice is yours. You can choose to use an end-to-end solution, build everything from scratch or mix and match. Regardless of your choice, the principles and techniques discussed here will be a valuable tool in your arsenal.

Of course, there are a lot of things that we haven't covered here. It isn't possible to present the entire spectrum of ML infrastructure in a single book. Because, in a sense, this is equivalent to presenting the entire spectrum of software infrastructure.

So where to go from here? In my mind, you have two choices:

- Keep learning by reading more books and watching more courses.
- Tackle a real-life problem and build a machine learning application.

If you go with the first option, I'm sure you will find many resources to continue your journey. One excellent stop is our blog, AI Summer, where we are constantly publishing new articles around deep learning.

However, I'm a big advocate of the second choice. Software engineering is one of those fields that can never be mastered unless you get your hands dirty and build real things. No book can give you the experience you'd acquire once you've developed and deployed your own project. Even if it is just a toy example with no real-world purpose. Try to experiment with different solutions, get to know their pros and cons. Read and try to replicate open-source code, familiarize yourself with different patterns. Then, you will have all the necessary skills to advance your career, either by joining a tech company or by founding your own AI start-up.

By reading and understanding everything we talked about, you already have a significant advantage over other machine learning engineers. You stand at the intersection of machine learning and software engineering because you possess skills from both fields.

But even if you are committed to the academic space, you now have a clear image of what it takes to build AI products and how to utilize this knowledge to advance your research.

I am truly honoured that you chose this book and I hope that I didn't let you down. If you leave with a slightly better understanding of the area, I consider this a success. Feel free to share it with people who might be interested. Also, don't hesitate to contact me for whatever questions or remarks you might have.

It's been a pleasure. Adios...

Appendix

AI Summer	theaisummer.com/
Docker	docs.docker.com/
Docker Compose	docs.docker.com/compose/
Flask	flask.palletsprojects.com/en/2.0.x/
Git	git-scm.com/doc
Google Cloud	cloud.google.com/docs
Kubernetes	kubernetes.io/docs/home/
Nginx	nginx.org/en/docs/
NumPy	numpy.org/doc/
Python	docs.python.org/3/
Tensorflow	www.tensorflow.org
Tensorflow Extended	www.tensorflow.org/tfx
uWSGI	uwsgi-docs.readthedocs.io/en/latest/
Vertex AI	cloud.google.com/vertex-ai/docs

List of Figures

Index

About the Author

Sergios Karagiannakos is a Machine Learning Engineer with a focus on ML infrastructure and MLOps.

He is based in Athens, Greece and graduated with a Master's in Electrical and Computer Engineering from University of Patras. He has helped several companies build their Artificial Intelligence products; most notably, Eworx SA where he joined as a Data Scientist, and Hubspot as part of the Machine Learning infrastructure team.

In 2019, he founded AI Summer, an educational platform around Deep Learning. During this time, he has authored more than 50 articles and he published the Introduction to Deep Learning & Neural Networks course.

Interesting facts: He was included in the Top 100 influential voices and brands in Data Science and Deep Learning, he strives to bring the entire Greek tech community together, and he really wishes that Artificial General Intelligence will be solved in our lifetime.

Printed in Great Britain
by Amazon

86899024R00127